PYRAMID POWER

A comprehensive and fascinating guide to pyramids – their origins, secret purposes, and the many incredible uses to which the mysterious energies they generate can be put.

PYRAMID POWER

The secret energy of the ancients revealed

by

MAX TOTH and GREG NIELSEN

DESTINY BOOKS
NEW YORK

Destiny Books
377 Park Avenue South
New York, New York 10016

First Quality Paperback Edition 1985

10 9 8 7 6 5 4 3 2 1

LIBRARY OF CONGRESS CATALOGING IN PUBLICATION DATA

Toth, Max.
  Pyramid power.

  Bibliography: P.
  Includes index.
  1. Pyramids — Miscellanea.   I. Nielsen, Greg.
II. Title.
BF1999.T64   1985   001.9   85-15912
ISBN 0-89281-106-4 (Pbk.)

Destiny Books is a division of Inner Traditions International Ltd.

Printed and bound in Great Britain

Contents

To the two
NANCYS

Acknowledgements

Our extreme gratitude and appreciation first goes to Karl Drbal of Prague, Czechoslovakia. Chapter 8, exclusively written, is the first publication of his to appear in the United States. Expertly using wit and humour to describe his technical research into Pyramid Energy, his contribution answers many questions of long standing and adds a finishing touch to the completion of our book.

We are grateful to the authors, G.S. Pawley and N. Abrahamsen, and to *Science* for permission to reprint the article, 'Do the Pyramids Show Continental Drift?', originally published in *Science*, Vol. 179, pp. 892-893, 2 March 1973 and copyrighted 1973 by the American Association for the Advancement of Science.

Many thanks are extended to Henry Monteith of Albuquerque, New Mexico, for his superb contribution to Chapter 7; Joan Ann De Mattia, of New York City, for her enjoyable narration of how she put pyramid energy to work for her, Chapter 12; Robert Cousins, architect, for his valuable plans and illustrations; Manly P. Hall for permission to quote from his book *The Secret Teachings of all Ages*; Dr Boris Vern for his preliminary research findings and graphic illustrations; and to Al Manning, director of the E.S.P. Laboratory.

In addition, our thanks go to Renee Felice and Lynn Wilkens for their invaluable assistance in the preparation of this book.

Finally, though equally important, we appreciate the voluminous material contributed by innumerable books, publications, organizations and individuals.

Foreword

Much that has been considered the superstition of past civilizations is now proving to be the core of an ancient secret science; many a modern discovery betrays its origin and basis in this secret science. Certainly, pyramid power is at the forefront of these rediscoveries.

In 1968, Nobel Prize winner Dr Luis Alvarez set out to scientifically solve some of the mysteries of the pyramid; specifically to discover any secret chambers or passages in the Chephren's Pyramid of Giza. By the time his project got under way, thousands of scientists from all over the world had become involved. In order to attain his goal, Alvarez decided to use a new method of measurement; he measured the bombardment of cosmic rays passing through more or less dense objects. After measuring over two million rays, he had the tapes run through a computer in Cairo. Nothing out of the ordinary showed up.

A short time later, however, John Tunstall, a reporter from *The Times*, in an article dated 14 July 1969, quoted one of the scientists in charge of the project, as saying, 'It defies all known laws of physics'. It seems that the tapes had been run through several computers; each more modern than the last. And each time the tapes were run through a new computer, a different pattern would emerge.

'This is impossible,' the scientist, Dr Amr Gohed, told the reporter.

The Times' reporter then asked: 'Has all the scientific know-how been rendered useless by some force beyond man's comprehension?'

The scientist replied, 'Either the geometry of the pyramid is in substantial error, which would affect our readings, or there is a mystery which is beyond explanation — call it what you will, occultism, the curse of the pharaoh, sorcery or magic; there is some force that defies the laws of science at work in the pyramid.'

To the average reader, this statement must have seemed almost laughable. After all, pyramids have hardly been a subject of intensive

interest to most people. In school, students read about them briefly in
their history books; they study them as a geometric form in their
mathematics classes – and they forget them as soon as they walk out
of the classrooms in which they have just taken their final
examinations.

The average adult has seen photo essays about pyramids in
magazines such as *Life* and *National Geographic*; some have even
seen documentary films or travelogues which include sequences on the
pyramids of Egypt. But only a few people have any idea of the impact
which pyramids have had on the growth of civilizations; even smaller
is the group of people that believes, like Dr Gohed, 'that there is some
force that defies the laws of science at work in the pyramid'. We are
members of that group and it is because of our belief in the power of
the pyramids that this book was written. For, although there are many
books about the pyramids of Egypt, there are very few about the
lesser-known pyramids of the world and none, that we know of, about
the power of the pyramidal shape.

In the early 1970s, numerous magazines, including *Time, Esquire,
Playgirl, Psychic Observer, Probe the Unknown, Spaceview*, and *Your
Personal Astrology* all published articles on what is popularly called
'pyramid power'. We have followed up on many of these stories and
have learned that experimentation is going on, both in scientific
laboratories and home workshops. The contents of this book include
some of the results of these fascinating experiments. In addition we
suggest a number of simple experiments for the reader in his home
which scientists have performed in their laboratories. Since pyramid
research is becoming more widespread new advances are being made
all the time. *Pyramid Power* offers the most up to date source material
available in the field of pyramidology.

The book is divided into two parts so that each part may be read
independently of the other. Part I penetrates the secrets of pyramid
structures that remain standing to this day, even though they were
constructed *thousands* of years ago. The ancient civilizations of Peru,
Central America, and Egypt all turned their religious devotion toward
the mystery surrounding the pyramids. Part II investigates the powers
of the pyramid being researched in occult and scientific circles. The
sharpening of razor blades, the preservation of foodstuffs, the pyramid
as a generator of spiritual energies and other amazing powers are
explored. Also there is an exclusive paper by Karl Drbal, a Czech,
who took out the original pyramid patent.

All in all there is much mystery, fantasy, legend and conjecture associated with the modern conception of the pyramids.

We herewith invite you to join with us in investigating the mysteries of the pryamids old and new — construct your own miniature pyramid (instructions in Chapter 11) and investigate for yourself the mysterious energies focused in and around pyramidal structures.

PART 1
BENEATH THE SANDS:
THE ARCHAEOLOGIST'S
PYRAMID

1

A Falcon's-eye View of the Pyramid

Pyramids! The word evokes an image of immense structures soaring upward from a vast ocean of sand — three massive triangular-faced monuments and a huge half-human, half-animal statue — arbitrarily grouped together, parched by a searing sun and eroded by relentless winds.

These are the pyramids of Egypt — tangible enigmas, ancient remnants of a time beyond memory, beyond history, beyond understanding. Like lesser-known pyramids in other parts of the world, these colossal architectural edifices have, over the centuries, provided archaeologists, historians and mystics with material for thousands of volumes, numberless theories, endless debates, and inner meditations.

Today, the mysteries still continue to intrigue and plague scientists, scholars, and all those forever searching the mysteries. *Who built the pyramids? For what purpose? From where did the unknown builders acquire the extraordinarily advanced scientific and astronomical knowledge used to design these mammoth structures? And with what elaborate and complex technological equipment were these edifices created?*

These questions, while still unanswered, continue to pique the imaginations and curiosities of many. Theories have been developed by the score — some highly bizarre, some remarkable only for their lack of intelligent consideration of the historical context with which the theorists are dealing — books have been written, documentary and fictional films have been made, all dealing with the ever-fascinating subject of the pyramids. And although none of these authors, theorists or cinematographers has, to the best of our knowledge, come any closer than their curious predecessors of a thousand years ago to uncovering the secrets of the pyramids, still the search goes on.

During the past hundred years, pyramids have been recorded with varying degrees of accuracy as to location. Most of these have been sighted by military pilots flying over uncharted areas during their flight missions. Although a few of these unusual pyramids have been photographed, some of the pictures, it seems, were subsequently lost or misplaced. Attempts to verify the existence of the rediscovered structures have been discouraged by impassable terrains and, ultimately, reports have depended entirely on eyewitness accounts and recording the legend of the natives close to the region.

Pyramids of the World

A big complex of pyramid structures with one large pyramid is apparently located in the Shensi province of China. The complex is situated many miles west of the ancient Chinese capital of Sian-fu, a walled city older than Peking. The main pyramid is said to be well over a thousand feet high and surrounded, within miles, by an unspecified number of flat-topped pyramids all of which are allegedly aligned to true north. The Shensi pyramids seem to be constructed from a mixture of lime and clay, hardened into a cement-like material; they are covered with casing stones and decoratively painted in various colours.

Another Asiatic pyramid is located somewhere in the Himalayan Mountains. It is called the white pyramid and is described as shimmering white, encased in metal or some sort of stone, with a huge capstone made of a jewel-like material, possibly a crystal.

In the jungles of Cambodia lie the ancient ruins of the once great city, now known as Angkor, which contained splendid temples, endless galleries and vast pyramids. Cambodian history tells nothing of the origin of this sacred city. The oral tradition handed down through generations of Cambodians tell us only that it was either the work of giants or that of Pra-Eun, known as the king of angels. Although the imposing temple of Angkor Vat, the main structure in the abandoned city, was studied and partly restored before the Indo-Chinese conflict, very little is known about the local pyramids, except that their general proportions are similar to the Egyptian ones.

A complex of pyramids was reported to have existed in a desert region in the central Siberian uplands, north of Olekminsk. Eye-witness accounts claim that a Soviet aerial armada consisting of bombers and fighter planes literally blasted the desert region from the face of the earth. This bombardment, which allegedly occurred in the spring of 1970, is said to have wiped out a flying saucer base but, because there was no mention of this incident in the Soviet press, all reports of the incident are regarded as gossip and will remain shrouded in mystery until the true story is known.

Western Europe has its share of pyramid-like structures too. One such structure we found in the south of France. It is thought that this pyramid was built by the Knights Templar upon their return from the Crusades. Beneath it is a subterranean pit with astrological symbols carved into the walls.

Silbury Hill, in Wiltshire, is one of many British cone-shaped mounds or stepped earthen pyramids. This hill is believed to have been constructed over 4000 years ago. The builders used approximately a million tons of earth, spreading it out over a five-acre base and stacking it more than 150 feet high. Ancient graves, capped with an earthen structure similar to Silbury Hill, have been found in Ireland.

Usage of small pyramidal or conical markers for graves and for unknown religious ceremonies seems to have been a widespread phenomena in the Western Hemisphere where, especially in the United States, many such mini-pyramids have been found. For example, near the small community of Williams, Montana, is a series of three-foot tall pyramids. The Montana Historical Society reports that these are possibly markers for some unknown band of shepherds. This explanation does not seem to be completely acceptable, however. Even though these mini-pyramids were constructed along a northwest-southwest line, following the course and direction taken by the sheepherders, they appear to be several thousands of years old, and pre-date the appearance of the sheepherders by centuries.

Another site, at Painted Rock Reservoir near Gila Bend, Arizona, was found in 1959 by archaeologists from the University of Arizona. This small, flat-topped pyramid mound, dated between A.D. 900 and 1150, is thought to have been used by American Indians for religious purposes.

A large pyramid mound in Collinsville, Illinois is gaining notoriety as anthropologists dig deeper into a mysterious massive earthen mound at Cahokia Mounds State Park. The Cahokia mound has a base larger than the Great Pyramid in Egypt, measuring 1000 feet wide and 800 feet long, and presently estimated to be about 100 feet high. The pyramid mound is part of a tremendous complex of ruins at Cahokia which contains a great wall and sacrificial pits built by a lost Indian civilization. The experts estimate that over 20 million cubic feet of earth were moved to the site during a period of 250 years. Archaeologists say that the Cahokia pyramid is the largest prehistoric structure in the United States and that the Cahokians reigned for at least 500 years with colonies as far as 1000 miles from their city.

Rumours, dating back dozens of years, establish pyramids in Alaska, Florida, within the boundaries of the world famous Bermunda Triangle, the lost continent of Atlantis and other spots underneath the Atlantic and Pacific oceans. These rumours, currently dismissed as folklore, may some day be granted further credence, or even scientific validity through a chance discovery by an adventurer or soldier of fortune, or by the painstaking revelation of an archaeological expedition.

Seemingly, the only geographical locations on earth devoid of pyramidal structures are Australia and the Antarctic region. But archaeological research may yet reveal pyramids in these regions – pyramids enveloped, as are those in Central and South America, by natural growth. There is also the possibility that new pyramids will be unearthed near present locations of stone and earth mounds.

Certainly, any archaeological expedition which unearthed a new pyramidal site would win worldwide attention and acclaim. This is because pyramids are today the subject of a great deal of interest – not merely from archaeologists, but also in scientific and para-psychological circles.

It should be noted here that to determine the date of an archaeological find, excavators all over the world have been using the analysis of radioactive carbon, the isotope Carbon 14. Unfortunately, it now appears that the dates obtained through the use of this method are highly questionable, since contamination from present day organic materials could substantially affect the process. Archaeologists now believe that most of the sites dated with Carbon 14 are actually older than the dating process showed that they were. There is currently an enormous controversy raging in archaeological circles over the claim of some archaeologists that Carbon 14 dating is incorrect by thousands of years, not hundreds as was previously thought.

Despite the now-apparent flaws in what has, for the past several decades, been accepted as a valid, scientific dating method, Carbon 14 is still useful in that it provides us with information about the evolution and succession of civilizations. Therefore for the sake of convenience, in this and other chapters dealing with archaeological finds, the dates provided by the Carbon 14 process will be used to provide readers with a reference point.

Origin of the Word 'Pyramid'

There is a great deal of mystery surrounding pyramids – from the enigma of the building to the colossal Egyptian, Mayan and Peruvian pyramids to the perplexing and inexplicable powers seemingly intrinsic to the pyramidal shape. And perhaps the first mystery of the pyramids is that of the origin of the name itself.

Obviously, the English word is derived from the Greek *PYRAMIS* (plural *pyramides*). Less obvious is the derivation of the Greek word itself. It does not seem to be derived from *MR* (pronounced *mer*), the Egyptian word for the four-sided, triangular-faced, square-based structure. (To add to the confusion, this Egyptian word has, itself, no descriptive significance, according to I.E.S. Edwards in *The Pyramids of Egypt*.)

One possible ancestor of *pyramis* is a word found in the Rhind Mathematical Papyrus, now in the British Museum. This word, *PER-EM-US*, is described in the Egyptian mathematical treatise as indicating the vertical height of a pyramid. Literally translated, it means 'what goes (straight) up ...' (from something, signified by the final syllable *US*). Unfortunately, the meaning of this syllable is not known and therefore the word is only partially clear.

To accept the explanation that *pyramis* is actually derived from *per-em-us* would be to imply that the Greeks either misunderstood the meaning of the Egyptian term or, by the linguistic process known as *synecdoche*, named the entire pyramidal structure after the Egyptian word for a part of it. Egyptologists, finding this explanation unacceptable, have accepted the term *pyramis* as a purely Greek word with no known connection with Egyptian terminology.

It has been suggested that the Greeks facetiously chose this word because it means, in their language, 'wheaten cake', and, when seen from a distance, the pyramids did, indeed seem to them to resemble large cakes. Another example of the Greek custom of humorously applying a descriptive word from their own language to an object having no exact parallel in their own architecture, is *obeliskos*, which now means obelisk, but which also means 'a little spit, or skewer'.

An entirely different derivation is suggested by Gerald Massey in *Ancient Egypt: The Light of the World*. Massey traces the word back to the Greek *PUR* (pronounced *pyr*) meaning 'fire' and the Egyptian *MET*, meaning 'ten', or 'a measure'. Thus, he asserts, the word stands for the ten original measures or arcs traced by the god of fire, the sun, through the zodiacal circuit. Since the Great Pyramids at Gizeh, among others, seem to have been constructed according to sidereal measurements, this theory is plausible. The word would then literally mean, 'a ten-form measure of fire', a symbolic figure for manifest life.

Motives for Building

The controversy over the derivation of the word *pyramid* is minor compared to that which rages over the purpose of the pyramids themselves. Egyptologists claim that the pyramids were tombs; Peruvianists and other archaeologists investigating in Meso-America state that they were used as temples. And some pyramidologists now believe that the pyramids are, possibly, resonators or storehouses of energy. Their finding is that the frequencies radiated by the earth itself (including the magnetic force lines) and cosmic radiation blend within the pyramidal structure and produce a beat frequency (in the same way in which two piano keys, when struck simultaneously, produce a third, or beat frequency). This beat frequency, they suggest, could create an energy radiation.

The question then becomes: were the pyramids built precisely for the purpose of storing, or producing, energy? If so, for what purpose were they used? And how did the architects learn that pyramids could be used in such a manner?

There is no doubt that every civilization which built pyramids did so with the use of highly advanced mathematical and astronomical calculations and a seemingly impossible mastery of the skill of stone masonry. In civilizations separated not only by thousands of miles but also by hundreds of years, stones weighing many tons were hoisted into position with infinite precision for the purpose of erecting pyramidal structures. Because of the virtually identical use of skill and science in the erection of the pyramids, it is impossible not to conjecture that perhaps these skills and sciences were taught to the pyramid builders by persons from *outside* the civilizations. If so, from where did these outsiders come? How did they get here? Did they teach astronomy and mathematics for the sole purpose of having the pyramids constructed? Or was there some other motive behind the endowment of this knowledge upon the peoples of the ancient civilizations?

Of course, there are at present no answers to these questions. Perhaps some day archaeologists will uncover written records which will, at last, lay the mystery of the pyramids to rest. But until then, archaeologists will go on believing, as they have for centuries, that the

pyramids were built as temples or tombs. Beyond that unsupp
official explanation, the curious mind will continue its investiga
into one of the most fascinating architectural enigmas of all times.

2

The Pyramids of Peru

Although civilization in Peru apparently began before 9000 B.C., it was not until 1940 that archaeologists began for the first time to unearth the secrets of this great pre-Columbian civilization. Subsequent archaeological excavation has revealed buildings with construction features similar to those of the pyramidal structures still extant in Peru. These early pre-pyramids were probably built around 1300 B.C., some 1500 years before the erection of the enormous and magnificent Peruvian pyramids of approximately A.D. 200.

The great and rather sudden cultural advances which occurred around 1300 B.C. seem to have coincided with the appearance of the highly developed *Chavin* civilization whose influence is thought to have been spread by the vogue of a new religious cult. This civilization, which is named after the ceremonial centre situated at Chavin de Huantar in the northern Peruvian highlands, close by the Marañon River, is probably the foundation stone on which other, later Peruvian cultures were built.

According to Peruvianists (archaeologists who are concerned exclusively with Peruvian excavation) the site at Chavin de Huantar is the largest and most important of the few typical sites known to us. There is speculation that the site's stone buildings, containing many rooms not well suited for habitation, possibly comprised a ceremonial centre much like the Mayan ceremonial centres, also composed of stone buildings, in Central America.

Unfortunately, this site has never been completely investigated. Because of the stones and other debris which filled many of the rooms and galleries of its most important building, archaeologists were unable to fully explore the structure or to make a detailed plan of it. It now appears that further investigation may be impossible, since the Chavin site was almost completely inundated by a massive landslide in 1945. However, archaeological exploration prior to 1945 did yield the information that the Chavin complex covers an area of over 800 feet and is completely landscaped. Because of its highland location, the ancient complex was untouched by such natural destructive agents as tropical vegetation and harsh drifting sands. The sunken courts, raised platforms, terraces, plazas and stone edifices, all oriented to the cardinal points, remained virtually intact, eroded neither by time nor nature.

The most impressive and well preserved of all the buildings at Chavin de Huantar is the Castillo, or castle, which far exceeds the other structures in size and importance.

The Castillo is an immensely complex building, seemingly pre-pyramidal in structure. Its base measures 245 feet by 235 feet and is, like the base of most pyramids, almost square. It stands approximately 45 feet high; its outer walls slope slightly inward toward the top and are set back in several narrow terraces, highly reminiscent of the Egyptian step Pyramids.

Remarkably advanced in architectural concept, the castle was evidently well planned before construction, and was obviously built by masons of considerable experience.

The interior of the Castillo has many of the features of the famous Egyptian Pyramid. It has three floors of dry stone masonry with ventilating shafts running horizontally and vertically. So well planned and constructed were these shafts that they still provide fresh air for the interior of the castle. The huge thick walls were built from split stones and are filled with rubble. The outer walls are surfaced with large, rectangular finished stones laid alternately thick and thin.

The interior has a typically pyramidal labyrinth of walls, galleries, rooms, stairs and ramps. The galleries are about 3 feet wide; the rooms range from 6 to 16 feet in width. Both rooms and galleries are less than 6 feet high and are of less cubic area than the walls and remaining masonry. There is no lighting except that afforded by the ventilating shafts. The only exterior opening is the main entrance, which is reached by a stairway of cut rectangular stones.

Another smaller site built in the pre-pyramidal architectural tradition of Chavin is at Wilkawain, near Huaraz, in the northern highlands of Peru. The Wilkawain complex consists of a stone temple and several one- and two-storey stone houses. The temple is a small replica of the Castillo at Chavin. This mini-castle measures about 35 feet by 52 feet and, like the Castillo, has three stories of interior ramps, staircases, galleries, rooms and ventilating shafts. Each floor

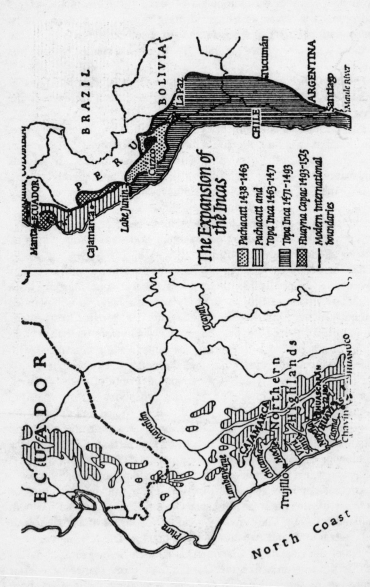

The Expansion of
the Incas

Pachacuti 1438-1463

Pachacuti and
Topa Inca 1463-1471

Topa Inca 1471-1493

Huayna Capac 1493-1525

Modern international
boundaries

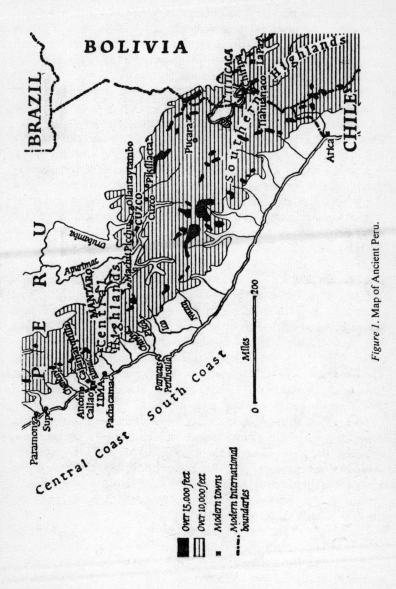

Figure 1. Map of Ancient Peru.

contains seven principal rooms, larger than those of the Castillo, measuring 7 by 22 feet wide and over 6 feet high. The roof is gabled with great slabs placed on a slope, and is covered with stones and dirt in such a way as to produce a domed effect. This castle is not as famous as the one at Chavin de Huantar; like its better-known namesake, it has never been fully explored because of the stones and other debris which completely clog some of its rooms.

The Chavin culture spread throughout Peru and prospered for several thousand years. During this time a religious cult arose which required community erection of temples and other religious structures. The most prominent of the deities to which the cult paid tribute was a feline, a puma or jaguar, whose name is unknown to Peruvianists. Also unknown to the experts is the exact purpose of the complexes at Chavin and Wilkawain. It has been suggested that the Castillo was a shrine to which pilgrimages were made from a large surrounding region. Another theory is that the complexes were centres at which the entire population gathered on specific occasions, such as ceremonial celebration days or market days.

The Moche Culture

The growth of the Chavin culture seems to have halted, as abruptly as it started, some time around 300 B.C. The culture of Peru then stagnated for about five centuries, until approximately A.D. 200, when two new cultures appeared almost simultaneously. These two civilizations, that of the *Moche* on the northern coast of Peru and the *Tiahuanaco*, or Wari-Tiahuanaco, in the southern highlands, seem to have emerged virtually full-blown; they both reached the height of their magnificance by approximately A.D. 600.

The people of the Moche civilization erected many massive and impressive temples, the most famous of which are the gigantic twin pyramids at Moche, close by the modern city of Trujillo. These twin pyramids are known today as 'La Huaca del Sol' (The Temple of the Sun) and 'La Huaca de la Luna' (The Temple of the Moon). Each consists of a massive terraced platform of adobe. The temple of the sun even has a terraced pyramid on its platform.

The Temple of the Sun is the most immense structure on the coast of Peru. The platform rises in five terraces to a height of 60 feet; its base measures 450 feet by 750 feet. On the top of the fifth terrace is a causeway nearly 20 feet wide and 300 feet long which leads to the north end of the pyramid. A 340-foot square and 75-foot high stepped pyramid surmounts the platform at the southern end. The entire Huaca del Sol is estimated to contain at least 130 million adobe bricks.

Although the platform of the Temple of the Moon is much smaller at the base than that of the Temple of the Sun – it measures only 195 feet by 260 feet – it is approximately 10 feet higher than the Temple of the Sun. On the top of the platform of the Huaca de la Luna some rooms with frescoed walls in typical Moche design and colours still remain.

Just south of Lima, Peru, another Moche pyramid stands. This is the great pyramidal temple of Pachacamac, which overshadows the city in the Lurin Valley. The Pachacamac temple covers approximately 12 acres of ground and rises nearly 75 feet high. So famous was this shrine in Inca and pre-Inca days that at the time of the Spanish conquest, it was considered the mecca of Peru.

Tiahuanaco

Mystery shrouds the ruins of Tiahuanaco, the last vestiges of a culture which, even at its nascence rivalled the culture of the Moche. There are some who claim that Tiahuanaco is the birthplace of the Americas; and possibly even the world's civilization. One theory suggests that Tiahuanaco was originally an island which first sank into the Pacific Ocean and was then uplifted with the Andes to its present height. Another hypothesis holds that Tiahuanaco was the seat of a powerful and megalithic empire ruling the entire world.

Tiahuanaco is situated at an altitude of 13,000 feet, a dozen miles south-east of Lake Titicaca, the world's highest navigable lake. With its extremely thin atmosphere, cold climate and nearly treeless surroundings, Tiahuanaco hardly seems a likely candidate for the birthplace of a civilization. Yet despite the uninviting surroundings (most people have trouble breathing in this rarified atmosphere), or perhaps because of them, many mystics the world over consider Tiahuanaco to be a truly holy site.

It is interesting to note at this point, a story about the Creator god worshipped at Tiahuanaco who was called Viracocha and in many respects resembles the Mexican god Quetzalcoatl. Ancient lore states that after travelling through the country instructing his people, Viracocha set off across the Pacific, from the shores of Ecuador, walking on the waves!

The masonry at Tiahuanaco is the best and most monumental in the Andean region. There are four large buildings and a number of smaller ones on the site, altogether occupying approximately 1475 feet by 3275 feet, or one-sixth of a square mile.

The largest building at Tiahuanaco is the Acapana, a 50-foot high terraced pyramid which was originally faced with stone. The irregular ground plan of the Acapana measures approximately 690 square feet.

The best known structure at Tiahuanaco is the world famous Gateway of the Sun. This is a great monolithic gateway sculpted from a single, enormous block of andesite. Unquestionably one of the archaeological wonders of the Americas, the Gateway is 10 feet high, $12\frac{1}{2}$ feet wide, and weighs an estimated 10 to 15 tons.

Researchers believe that the Tiahuanacoans also built the great wall at Sacsahuaman, near the city of Cuzco. Actually consisting of three terraced walls, the structure reaches a total height of 60 feet and stretches for more than 1800 feet (nearly half a mile). The walls are built of monolithic blocks of stone and traverse a zig-zagged route rather than a straight line. It is extremely interesting to note that the masonry of these walls is extremely reminiscent of that of the walls of the Egyptian pyramids. One of the points of similarity is in the fact that the stones in the walls, like those in the pyramids, have been fitted so precisely that a razor or other thin-edged blade cannot be slipped between the blocks. Another similarity is that the stones in both the wall and the pyramids were jig-sawed into place without the use of mortar. Also in the construction of both the pyramids and the wall, massive stones were used; one of the largest stones in the wall is reported to be 10 feet wide, 17 feet high, 9 feet thick, and well over 100 tons in weight. One difference in the construction of the two structures is that the workmen who built the wall bevelled the edges of all the blocks of stone, apparently for artistic effect. One of the stones in the wall is so exquisitely chiselled that it has become world-famous as the 'Stone of Twelve Angles'.

Nazca

Another mysterious site is Nazca, situated on the southern coast of Peru. At one time a densely occupied area whose actual dimensions are not on record, the Nazca site contains a unique area called *La Estaqueria*, or *the place of stakes*, which is best described as a wooden Stonehenge. It is a level sandy area with large quantities of tree trunks planted in orderly rows and masses. The greatest number of twelve rows of twenty trunks each is arranged into a quadrangle. Most of the single posts seemed to have been used as columns. They have forked tops and possibly supported a roof. Amazingly, the wood is still firm and hard, although it has been exposed to the elements for thousands of years.

The Incas

The Moche and Tiahuanaco civilizations, like the Chavin civilization before it, seems to have come to an abrupt halt. Again, there was a long culturally stagnant period in Peru and again, a new culture burst forth, almost full-blown, as if it had been developed elsewhere and been transported, in its maturity, to Peru. This new empire was that of the Inca. In a period of little over 300 years, from circa A.D. 1200 to 1534, thirteen Incan emperors were to extend the domination of their civilization over an estimated 350,000 square miles; this empire covered nearly 3000 miles − from what is known today as central Chile to northern Ecuador.

Upon the death of an Incan emperor, elaborate funeral ceremonies were observed throughout the empire. Like those of the Egyptian pharoahs, the emperor's body was preserved in the palace by an unknown process of mummification. His innards were removed and preserved in special containers and his body was wrapped in finest textiles. The mummy was thereafter waited upon as during life.

The Incan commoner was entombed much like the Egyptian, in a bee-hive-shaped tomb above the ground. The body, wrapped in textiles or skins, was placed inside in natal posture, seated with knees to chin. These tombs were made of rude stone masonry and clay and mud and the bodies dried without decomposition.

The Incas did not build pyramids. Rather, they apparently rebuilt the existing pyramids in every important Inca town, just as they enlarged the great ceremonial centres in the major cities to accommodate the religious requirements of the Inca empire. Today, the best built, and preserved, as well as the largest and most impressive buildings surviving from the ancient Peruvian civilizations, are those public edifices built by Incan government labour and planned by state architects.

The structures described in this chapter are virtually the only keys which Peruvianists have to the history of this ancient country. It is generally assumed that with the Spanish conquest of the Incan empire, any records of pre-Incan civilizations were destroyed. All extant records of the Incan empire and of the fables of its genesis, are those compiled by Spanish historians at the time of the conquest. If there were ever any written histories of the Chavin and other pre-Incan civilizations, these are now lost forever. All that remains are the great pyramids — tantalizing relics of great and glorious civilizations inexplicably cut down in their prime.

3

The Mayas Scale the Heights

As far as archaeologists can ascertain, the evolution of the great and ancient Peruvian civilizations was paralleled by the growth of amazingly similar civilizations in that part of Central America which is today known as Mexico. Although comparatively little is known about these civilizations, two facts are indisputable: both cultures produced extraordinarily massive and complex pyramidal structures, and both cultures relied heavily on astronomical calculations in the planning and erection of all of their architectural edifices. None of this would be very surprising except for the belief of archaeologists that both cultures were totally insular; it is contended that neither culture had even the slightest knowledge of the other.

Meso- (or middle) American civilization cannot be traced much farther back than 1500 B.C. Known as the civilization of the *Mayas*, this culture has, due to its elaborate structure and great complexity, challenged the imagination of explorer and scholar alike. Mystics theorize that the Mayas originated from the lost continents of Atlantis and Mu. Less fancifully, archaeologists and historians consider the Americas to be the Mayan place of origin and credit these people with carrying to a higher degree a civilization shared by their neighbours.

It is now believed that the earliest of the Mayan civilizations is that of the Olmecs, a people who lived and flourished in what is today known as southern Vera Cruz and Tabasco. Archaeological excavations at these sites have produced huge stone heads and religious and calandric formulae inscribed on stone stelae. The religious art of the Olmecs is notable for its portrayal of strange beings whose faces are either swollen and infantile or else grotesque visages of tiger-like monsters.

The dominant religious figure of the Olmecs is depicted as an old man, usually portrayed in a sitting position with his head bowed. Supported on his head and shoulders is a bowl, possibly used for

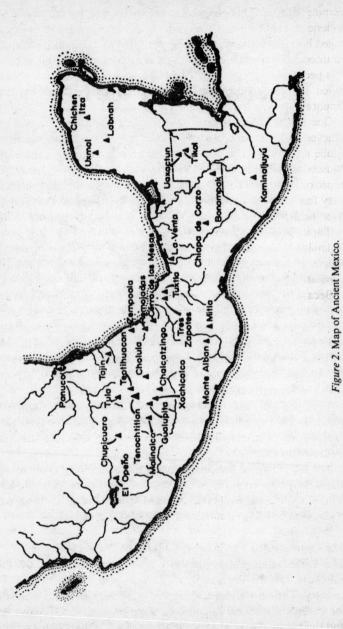

Figure 2. Map of Ancient Mexico.

burning incense. This god was to be worshipped by successive Meso-American civilizations. The Aztecs, of whom we will speak later, called him *Huehueteotl*, the old god, or *Xiuhtecuhtli*, lord of fire. Since Xiuhtecuhtli's worshippers dwelt in a volcanic region, this appellation was peculiarly appropriate. It has also been suggested that those who called him Huehueteotl identified him with the antiquity of the mountains in which they lived.

One of the most striking of all ancient Mexican religious sites is believed to have been built by the Olmecs. This is the massive oval adobe mound of Cuicuilco, built at the fringe of the volcanic range of Ajusco, at the south-west end of the Valley of Mexico. The mound is approximately 369 feet in diameter and has a wide ramp which soars sixty feet above the ground to the top of the structure. It is faced with river boulders, possibly to lessen the erosion of seasonal rains, or perhaps merely to enhance the effect of rugged majesty. The people of Cuicuilco built not a temple on the summit, but rather constructed a simple altar, exposed to both the elements and the eyes of the population.

Because of its soft lines and the lack of sharp corners and angles, the mound seems to be the spontaneous evocation of an immense religious spirit. In direct contrast is the altar. It has rectilinear, sloping walls with a pair of steps with vase-shaped rail supports. The sides of the altar are adobe faced and smooth, resembling the plasterwork of architecture developed more fully in religious edifices built centuries later in other parts of the world.

The people of Cuicuilco refurbished their religious building several times. Twice they replaced the altar by putting another one directly over the existing one. They even refaced the structure using sharp blocks of lava instead of the river boulders.

The beginning of the disappearance of the Olmec civilization was marked by the eruption of the volcano, Xitli, covering the bottom third of the mound with lava. It would appear that after this event, the civilization ceased to flourish and, in time, disappeared.

The Zapotecs and Teotihuacan Culture

The Olmec civilization seems to have been paralleled by that of Zapotecs, in the highlands of Oxaca, south-west of the Olmec country. Their art styles and writing were very different from that of the Olmecs. Calandric calculations were set forth in distinctive writing and their system fixed the date in terms of a fifty-two-year cycle.

The Zapotecs were very advanced, as is evidenced by their chief ceremonial site at Monte Alban. This covers a small mountain which is levelled and terraced into a gigantic natural platform. This in turn supports buildings such as temples and ball courts.

Like the Olmec, and other ancient American civilizations, the Zapotec civilization disappeared suddenly and inexplicably.

In approximately 600 B.C., a majestic ceremonial civilization known as Teotihuacan emerged. Situated in the valley of Teotihuacan, it is traditionally known as the 'place of the Gods'. In a vast area nearly 2 miles wide and $3\frac{1}{2}$ miles long, an imposing cluster of buildings are grouped. The floor of this zone was plastered, not once but many times. Obviously, it was neither an ordinary city nor simply a religious centre for temples and houses.

The architects planned and constructed their metropolis in several successive precincts extending southwards from the mighty Pyramid of the Moon. This was not a true pyramid but was truncated at the top to house a pyramid, and the faces of the platform were skillfully designed to provide terraces. From a rectangular court, a broad staircase led up the south side of the platform. Flanking the Plaza of the Moon were additional buildings; several hundred feet to the west and east, two smaller precincts added to the symmetry of the plan.

Two impressive rows of buildings of great size lead south from the Moon Plaza. Excavations of one revealed the contents, suggesting that it might have been the Temple of Agriculture. Smaller clusters of mounds lie off to the east. Directly to the south is a large unexcavated group of buildings and temples, called the 'Group of the Columns', because of some artifacts found in the vicinity.

The Pyramid of the Sun dwarfs all the other buildings in Teotihuacan. Like the Pyramid of the Moon, this massive pyramid is truncated at the top. Nearly 700 feet square at the base and in four terraces, it rises to over 200 feet. The faces of the pyramid were terraced by its builders to create the impression of even greater mass. The faces were also finished in stone with a covering of plaster, but the pyramid itself was built of adobe bricks.

The Pyramid of the Sun gives the illusion of infinite height and space. Cunningly calculated planes between its terraces are so designed that an observer standing at the base of the great staircase cannot see people at the top. When the stair was used during religious ceremonies, the effect must have been stupendous; the onlooker would have been conscious only of the elaborate procession of priests and officials disappearing into space as they ascended the stairs to encounter, unseen by the congregation, the infinity of the universe, and to be concentrated at the peak under the god's image.

The Pyramid of the Sun is constructed upon a wide platform built of square cells. The platform is walled in adobe and filled with refuse and rubble. Ruins suggest that the houses of priests may have lain outside of the pyramid on the platform. Extending southwards, smaller groups of mounds are found, consisting of several priestly dwellings and a minor temple clustered around a plaza. In one of these groups the floors are of mica, of which the ceremonial significance is unknown.

Across a river which ends in the south, lies a magnificent platform whose walls are faced with carved blocks and whose crowning pyramid temple has disappeared. It seems to have been built in honour of the rain god, Tlaloc, even though it is called the Temple of Quetzalcoatl.

The sacred city of Teotihuacan was consciously designed to convey the illusion of massiveness and eminence. It was constructed with buildings grouped along a north-south axis, laterally interrupted by precincts of edifices oriented along the east-west axis. From whatever angle Teotihuacan was approached, the eye was tastefully led towards a point of interest, guided by the arrangement of the plane and mass. The diminishing effect of distance was thus avoided. Within the precinct, the surrounding walls insulated the observer from the rest of the city, and consequently emphasized the enormity of each precinct temple.

Not even the Pyramids of Egypt were so carefully and consciously planned to lift the individual's soul by the sheer powers awakened by the place. One cannot escape the insistent association of ideas that the greater the temple, the more powerful the god for whom it was built.

Some time after the city of Teotihuacan was built, a mysterious renovation took place. Every building was rebuilt from the Pyramid of the Moon, at the north, to the Temple of Quetzalcoatl. Facades were covered up and rooms were filled in to create platforms of new pyramids. Not even the gigantic hulks of the Pyramid of the Sun and Moon escaped the addition of new stairs and facades. Strangely, the Temple of Quetzalcoatl underwent the most extreme alteration. This temple became the core for a high platform which supported a huge enclosure surrounded by a broad rampart. This rampart supported four lesser platforms on three of its sides. On the fourth side, the eastern wall, behind the main structure, three such temple foundations were built.

Although the reconstruction eventually extended to rebuilding the entire religious centre, no extreme shift in the styles of pottery or figurines suggests that the renovation was effected by another culture which had militarily conquered the Teotihuacanos. Instead, the new architecture has all the earmarks of a religious reformation which destroyed the symbolism of one cult to instill a new.

In the neighbourhood of Teotihuacan, some miles from the sacred city, tremendous communal dwellings were built, embracing fifty to sixty rooms set around patios connected by passageways. The rooms were built from adobe and rubblework, covered with plaster, and the inhabitants apparently enjoyed a life of comfort and security. There was also an altar prominently placed; religious rites were evidently not necessarily confined to the ceremonial site.

Teotihuacan had a great and pervasive influence on all of its neighbours. This is evidently in the Valley of Toluca, in Morelos, and abundantly in Puebla, where, at Cholula, the Teotihuacanos constructed an entire temple site of enormous extent. Excavation of this site has produced no carving as yet, but archaeologists have discovered one temple with a fresco decoration portraying the Butterfly God, a mythological being important to Teotihuacan religion.

The majestic city of Teotihuacan was rebuilt two more times. The renovation probably fulfilled the ceremonial requirements of rebuilding and refurbishing at the beginning, or ending, of a fifty-two-year cycle. The third rebuilding was done hastily and with maximum use of the original construction. This final rebuilding introduced new gods to be honoured and also heralded the end of the use of Teotihuacan as the sacred capital.

The Toltecs

The first people mentioned in the annals of the Valley of Mexico are the Toltecs of Tula, or master builders. These people appeared around A.D. 900 but their customs and achievements are so wrapped in the mystery which covers the facts of history, and so confusing and illogical are the references to them, that at one time their very existence was challenged by archaeologists.

The Toltecs have been described as brilliant architects, carpenters, mechanics and highly skilled agriculturists. They built their massive pyramids, palaces and houses of stone and mortar and used the *temascal*, or steam bath. They counted their years and used the sacred almanac of 260 days.

The history and remains of the Toltecs is as tenuous as their sociology and religion. One history, written by Ixtlilxochitl, begins with the creation of the world and the four suns, or eras, through which life has survived. The first era, the Water Sun, began when the supreme god, Tloque Nahuaque, created the world. Then, after 1716 years, or thirty-three 52-year cycles, it was destroyed by lightning and floods. The second era, the Sun of the Earth, saw the world populated by giants, called Quinametzin, who almost disappeared when earthquakes obliterated the earth. The Wind Sun came third, and the Olmecs, human tribes, lived on earth. The Olmecs destroyed the surviving giants, founded Cholula, and migrated as far as Tabasco. A spectacular individual, called Quetzalcoatl by some, Huemac by others, appeared in this era, bringing ethics and civilization. When the populace did not appear to benefit from his teachings, Quetzalcoatl returned to the east from whence he had come, prophesying as he went the destruction of the world by great winds and the conversion of humankind into monkeys. All of this, according to the narrative, came to pass. The fourth age, the present one, is called the Sun of Fire, and will end in a general conflagration. Such is the story of the Toltecs as set forth by Ixtlilxochitl.

The Toltec culture was highly cosmopolitan and although short-lived, established the structure of the tribute empire which the Aztecs later adopted. Its influence spread from one end of Meso-America to the other and is still particularly strong in Yucatan.

Because the Toltecs, like the peoples of other civilizations, built upon structures and, in turn, had their own structures built over by successive cultures, it is difficult to ascertain which pyramids and other edifices belong to which period. It is generally assumed that most of the Mexican pyramids were built by the Teotihuacanos or possibly by the people of a much earlier civilization.

The Aztecs

The last and greatest of the Mayan civilizations was that of the Aztecs which, archaeologists believe, had its probable source at Cholula, in the State of Puebla, where exists the largest structure in the world, in terms of cubic content.

As the archaeologists see it, Cholula was originally occupied by some unknown pre-classic people who later fell under the domination of the Teotihuacan civilization. At this time the inhabitants built a large ceremonial precinct, a maze of pyramidal temples, platforms and stairs, constructed of rubble and covered with plaster. Eventually some newcomers, possibly with the aid of the resident population, performed the stupendous task of converting the precinct into a single great platform, traditionally in honour of Quetzalcoatl. This mammoth construction entailed filling in every building and court-yard with adobe bricks. On the top they erected altars and quarters for the ceremonial clergy. In one of the altars, the Altar de los Craneos, two people were buried with a mortuary offering of pottery vessels which resemble those used by the Aztecs. Archaeologists, therefore, assume that in Puebla very possibly lies the source and inspiration of the Aztec civilization.

The Aztec civilization was brought to its greatest height by the Tenochcas, the Mexico City Aztecs, around A.D. 1400. Yet, according to authorities, the Tenochcas did not originate the civilization, or contribute much to it beyond the introduction of a sacrifice cult.

Like the people of all the great ancient civilizations, the Aztecs had a highly sophisticated knowledge of astronomy. The discovery of the Great Calendar Stone, built by Axayacatl, an Aztec chief, in A.D. 1479, convinced archaeologists that the Aztec knowledge of the science was even more refined than that of other civilizations. Based on an extremely involved mathematical and astronomical system, the Calendar Stone was incomprehensible until the discovery of the calendaric texts which not only led to an understanding of the meaning of the stone, but which aided in the deciphering of the Aztec hieroglyphics.

The Great Calendar Stone weighs over 20 tons, is 13 feet in diameter and was hewn from one monolithic block of stone. In the centre of the face of the Stone is the Sun God, Tonatiuh, flanked by four ornamental frames listing the four previous ages of the world. Added together, these represent the date of our present era. The central element is encircled by the names of the twenty days of the Aztec month. These in turn are ringed with a band of glyphs denoting jade or turquoise, symbolizing the heavens. This band is surrounded by the signs of the stars penetrated by the sun's rays in an emblematic design. Two immense fire serpents, symbolizing Year and Time, circle the exterior of the stone and meet, face-to-face at the base.

The Great Calendar Stone should be an enormous aid to

anthropologists and historians in the reconstruction of the chronological history of Meso-America. However, there are numerous opinions as to how the dates on the Stone should be correlated with Christian dates. Several calculations have been designed to reconcile the Aztec calendar with the Christian calendar, but each one involves an error of some 260 years in the expression of Aztec dating in Christian terms. This discrepancy has naturally led to many divergent interpretations of Meso-American chronology.

The source of civilization, as well as its disappearance, is always a mystery for archaeologists, anthropologists and historians, who rarely have access to historical records — only fragments of pottery and other artifacts from which they can construct vague theories. It is to be hoped that there will be further discoveries in Meso-America which, like the Great Calendar Stone and the calandaric texts, will shed light on the beliefs, and even the actions and motivations, of the people who built them. Certainly, until such discoveries are made, the mystery of the Meso-American pyramids will remain.

4

The Ancient Egyptians:
Pyramid Builders of the World

The Pyramid Age of Egypt began with the Third Dynasty and ended with the Sixth Dynasty. The dating of the thirty-one dynasties of the kings of Egypt in Manetho's *History of Egypt* has been generally accepted by Egyptologists. The thirty one dynasties have been grouped into nine main periods as a convenience in describing the most important changes undergone in Egyptian history.

The nine main periods of dynasties, with approximate dates are as follows:

3100-2686 B.C. – Early Dynastic Period	1st and 2nd Dynasties
2686-2181 B.C. – Old Kingdom	3rd to 6th Dynasties
2181-2133 B.C. – First Intermediate Period	7th to 10th Dynasties
2133-1786 B.C. – Middle Kingdom	11th and 12th Dynasties
1786-1567 B.C. – Second Intermediate Period	13th to 17th Dynasties
1567-1080 B.C. – New Kingdom	18th to 20th Dynasties
1080-664 B.C. – Late New Kingdom	21st to 25th Dynasties
664-525 B.C. – Saite Period	26th Dynasty
525-332 B.C. – Late Period	27th to 31st Dynasties

* According to I.E.S. Edwards in *The Pyramids of Egypt*.

During the Pyramid Age, approximately eighty pyramids were built. Many of the presently known pyramids have been reduced to nothing more than sand and rubble, but they are still recognizable by the archaeologist as once having been pyramids.

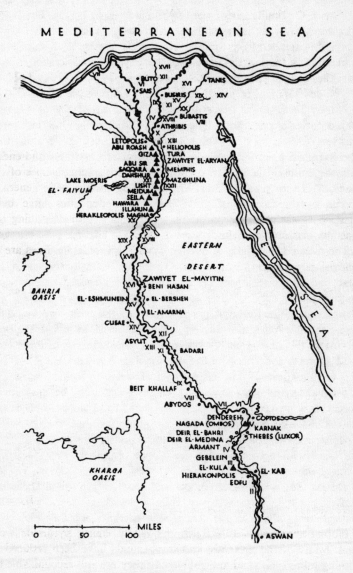

Figure 3. Location of Pyramids from Aswan to the Delta area.

Almost every pyramid was built on the fringe of the desert west of the Nile in the neighbourhood of Memphis. Memphis was probably designed as the seat of government by Menes, the first dynastic ruler of Egypt. Originally, there were two kingdoms in Egypt. The Upper Kingdom covered the area from Aswan to Memphis; the Lower Kingdom extended from Memphis to the Delta area. As tribute to the unification of the kingdoms by Menes, the pharaohs included in their titles that of 'King of Upper and Lower Egypt'.

The development of an official religion begins in the Pyramid Age. It is thought to derive from the cult (of unknown origin) of a temple with a powerful priesthood. The most sacred object within this temple was the *benben*, most probably a conically shaped stone thought to symbolize the primeval mound which emerged from primordial waters at the creation of the universe. These priests are credited with evolving nine deities known as the Great Ennead of Heliopolis.

The worship of two of these deities developed into cults, which exercised great influence on the religion of the pyramid builders: one was the sun cult and the other was the cult of Osiris. These were neither related in origin or in their main theological conception. Rē was primarily a god of the living; Osiris was basically the god of the dead and of the region of the dead. Both gods shared an important feature, that of survival after death. Osiris, after being murdered, was restored to life through magic. Rē, or the sun, whose daily disappearance past the horizon was considered as his death, was reborn as the sunrise each morning. In the experiences of these gods the Egyptians found reason to hope for their own survival. However, the continuation of life after physical death was not a natural consequence and was something which could only be assured by observing a proper ritual through which the dead were supplied with all the material help required by the gods for their own survival. According to Egyptologists, this is the basis for the need to provide the dead with a tomb and a burial conforming in every essential element with an accepted pattern.

Despite the exacting attention and detail given to all practical matters, the Egyptians never fully evolved a clear and exact conception of the after-life. They believed that each individual was composed of a body and a spirit, and that the spirit remained alive if the dead body was preserved and provided with necessary sustenance. They regarded the afterlife as a kind of mirror of this world. Where the spirits dwelt after life was unknown, but they are thought to have gone to a kind of underworld, the entrance to which was through the pit of the tomb, in which the dead were buried.

Pre-dynastic Burials

In pre-dynastic eras the dead were buried in oval or rectangular pits dug in the sand. The bodies were placed in fetal position, wrapped in a reed mat and laid on their sides. Then in the dynastic era, kings and nobles started building a *mastaba* over their graves. This is a superstructure of sun-dried mud brick placed over the burial pit.

Every *mastaba* was almost certainly a close copy of a house or a palace. It is probably for this reason that the tomb was regarded as the place where the dead dwelt. An interesting *mastaba* was discovered, in the 1950s, by W.B. Emery and dated to the reign of King Aha in the First Dynasty. Below the *mastaba*, was a shallow, rectangular pit divided into five compartments. The middle compartment is thought to have contained the body; the adjoining compartments probably housed the most intimate possessions. Above the pit the *mastaba* was divided into a rectangular twenty-seven celled interior, containing nine rows of three cells each. The outer walls of the superstructure were sloped inwards from the base to the truncated top. Corridors, usually provided to interconnect rooms, were considered unnecessary because it was thought that the spirit of the deceased could pass unhindered through any material barrier.

The Pyramid of Zoser

Until the end of the Second Dynastic Period, *mastabas* were built of brick, with some interior rooms lined with dressed stone. Then in the Third Dynasty, builders began to use stone for building the *mastabas* throughout. The first tomb to be constructed of stone is best known as the Step Pyramid. Its construction has been ascribed to King Zoser's architect, Imhotep, who is also credited with the invention of the art of construction in stone. Imhotep's name is on the pedestal of a statue found outside the tomb of Zoser when it was excavated, and thus indirectly confirms his connection with the tomb.

The achievements of Imhotep became a legend among Egyptians, who regarded him not only as an architect, but as the father of medicine, an accomplished astronomer and magician. Later generations of Egyptians deified him; the Greeks equated him with their own god of medicine.

The place which Imhotep selected to construct the pyramid was a stretch of high ground overlooking the city of Memphis, which measured about 1800 feet by 1000 feet, with its longest side oriented along the north-south axis. The step pyramid was the main, dominant feature of a big complex of buildings and courtyards, very much like those found in Peru and Mexico. The perimeter of the complex was enclosed with a massive stone wall.

Zoser's step pyramid is a massive construction, rising to a height of over 200 feet, in 6 steps, with a nearly square base of 411 feet by 358 feet. Apparently, like the Mayan pyramids, it underwent several changes of plan. The nucleus of the pyramid is a solid square structure consisting of a core of stone faced with an outer layer of dressed Tura limestone. This nucleus appears to have been a *mastaba* 26 feet high and about 207 feet square, aligned to the cardinal points (see Fig. 4).

The pyramid substructure contains a shaft 92 feet deep, leading to a maze of rooms and corridors, some of which were either not finished at the time of construction or were aborted additions of a later renovation. At the bottom of the shaft is the tomb chamber which is $5\frac{1}{2}$ feet high and wide, and $9\frac{3}{4}$ feet long, and completely built of pink granite from Aswan. At the northern end, in order to admit the body, a hole in the roof was bored. After the body was interred in the chamber, the hole was filled with one giant granite plug, 6 feet long and weighing about 3 tons.

The wall encircling the Step Pyramid complex was faced with dressed Tura limestone. It is about 33 feet high and the total length of it around the perimeter is over a mile.

Later generations of Egyptians regarded the Step Pyramid complex with esteem. This is evidenced by hieroglyphic graffiti on the passage walls of some of the attendant buildings in the court, which record the admiration felt by Egyptians who visited the complex a thousand years after its completion.

It is hard to believe that the degree of perfection of the architectural construction of Zoser's pyramid could have been achieved without being preceded by some lengthy process of development. Yet no evidence exists of the employment of stone in any earlier edifices except for a few isolated parts or sections of buildings. However, because small blocks were used in the construction of the Step Pyramid instead of the massive monolithic giant blocks employed in later construction efforts, it is believed that the technique of quarrying and manipulating massive pieces of stone may not yet have been mastered. This implication is a valid one from the point of view of the archaeologists. However, it does seem that Imhotep, with all his genius and inventiveness, was not masterful enough to develop the techniques necessary for this more sophisticated masonry accomplishment. Therefore, some Egyptologists theorize that for some unknown reason, large pieces of stone were not required, and that for this particular construction the smaller stones sufficed.

Very little remains of the enclosed complex surrounding the Step Pyramid, and even less awaited the archaeologists who entered and explored the various chambers; plunderers virtually denuded every artifact of any value. All that remained were tiled and reliefed walls, some empty coffins and a few pieces of human bone.

Zoser's successors followed the example he had set in building tombs in the form of a Step Pyramid, although they did not stress the importance of having a courtyard as the complex within the pyramid enclosure.

The Pyramids of Sekhemkhet and Khaba

Sekhemkhet, one of the kings succeeding Zoser, chose his site close to the original Step Pyramid complex. At the south-west corner of

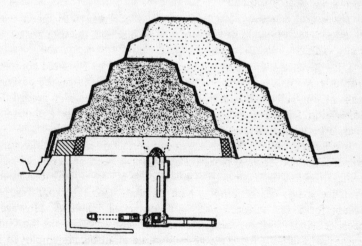

Figure 4. Plan of Step Pyramid.

Zoser's complex, Sekhemkhet laid out his enclosure about equal in length and about two-thirds in width. Planned on a base measuring about 395 feet square, the pyramid would have reached an estimated height of about 230 feet in seven steps, but because his reign lasted only six years, an unusually short period of time, much of the work was never completed. In later times the structure was used as a quarry, and it is now impossible to ascertain the height to which it was originally built.

Sekhemkhet's pyramid paralleled the interior of Zoser's, with a maze of corridors, rooms, blind doors and blind galleries. During the excavation of this pyramid in the early 1950s, the main corridor of the vertical shaft was discovered to have been still intact. Sealed in three places, the shaft led to the chamber corridor whose doorway to the burial chamber was still sealed with thick blocking walls of stone. No signs of tomb robbers was evident, and when the expedition led by Zakaria Goneim on behalf of the Service des Antiquites of the Egyptian Government, entered the burial chamber, they found a closed and sealed sarcophagus, on which a wreath had been placed. The sarcophagus, carved from a single block of alabaster, was very exceptional. Instead of having an entire top as a lid, one end of it was a sliding panel manipulated by a rope and pulley system. Plaster which had sealed the panel in its grooves after its ceremonial closure signified that it had not been disturbed since the time of the funeral. When the sarcophagus was finally opened – it was found to be empty! The deceptive indications of the shaft, burial chamber, and corridor and the missing mummy are a mystery which the archaeologists were hard put to explain. Naturally, more than one theory has been offered. One is that the body and its costly belongings were stolen by conniving priests and dignitaries in charge of the burial. The other is that the entire burial chamber was a dummy to protect the real location of the mummy which was buried in a still undisclosed tomb within the Pyramid or in another structure.

A third Step Pyramid, credited to an obscure king, called Khaba, is located in Zawiyet el-Aryan. This is not a true Step Pyramid but rather a layered one, hence the name, Layer Pyramid. Its superstructure covers an area of 276 feet square and though the structure was never completed it is probable that the architect planned to build it with six or seven steps.

The substructure differs in detail from the two previous pyramids, but in its surrounding complex, it is essentially identical to the others.

The absence of a sarcophagus and funerary equipment suggests that the pyramid was never used, and also that the construction never really reached an advanced stage.

In all three Step Pyramid complexes, nearly identical mortuary buildings were found in various stages of rubble. This could mean that the pyramid complex of Zoser's was so classical that the two subsequent architects decided to copy it exactly, only allowing themselves the privilege of modifying the substructure. It could also mean that there could have been a codex or master plan to follow in building the complex which was set down beforehand, and which succeeding architects had to follow. It is not known which theory is correct, but the latter explanation is less accepted. The master plan theory apparently has one confirming piece of evidence. This is in the shape of four small step pyramids situated several hundred miles up the Nile, in the vicinity of Thebes. Nothing is known with certainty about the history of these small pyramids. One of them, at El-Kula, was surveyed in 1949. It was then found that this pyramid was strangely oriented. Instead of each face being oriented to the cardinal points as is usual in most pyramids, each of the four corners is oriented to one of the four points.

The pyramid of El-Kula has only three steps and its base covers an approximate area of only 61 feet square. The substructures of these pyramids have not been found except for the one at Nagada. The substructure of this four-step pyramid is, simply, a pit dug very roughly from the rock and located directly beneath the centre of the pyramid. Since there is no tunnel or entrance to the outside of the pyramid face, it is assumed, that this is a tomb built so that access, following burial of the body, would be impossible. That is, they believe that the pit was dug, the body interred and the entire superstructure of the pyramid was then built around and on top of the tomb, sealing it from any possible later entry. Although when it was excavated, the substructure yielded no body, the stunned Egyptologists clung to their theory that the pit had been specifically designed as an impenetrable tomb.

Today the mystery of these four strangely located step pyramids remains. Could these pyramids possibly have been the models from which the actual pyramids in the Memphis region, several hundred miles further down the Nile, were planned or were they simply built by a group of renegade or outcast peoples who migrated to the vicinity of Thebes?

Evolution of the True Pyramid: Meidum

According to archaeologists, sometime at the end of the Third or the beginning of the Fourth Dynasty, a significant alteration occurred in the design of the step pyramid. The steps of the pyramid were filled in, producing four smooth faces and sloping inwards to a point at the summit, forming what has become classically known as the *true* pyramid.

Egyptologists believe that they have found the reason for the transition from the step pyramid to the true pyramid from investigations of the badly damaged pyramid at Meidum, about 30 miles south of Memphis. In its present condition this structure resembles a high rectangular tower rather than a pyramid.

The pyramid at Meidum is thought to have been patterned after Zoser's pyramid and seems to have undergone several trans-formations during its construction. After carefully perusing some drawings on rocks, and from observations made on the site, the Egyptologists came to the conclusion that the pyramid was first built with two, three and then four steps. After this stage it was enlarged to a seven-stepped structure, which was then enlarged to eight steps. The inclination of the steps were at 75 degrees and the finished pyramid base measures approximately 473 feet square, but the actual height it eventually reached is uncertain.

Apparently, the seven-stepped design was intended to be the finished pyramid; the eight-step pyramid was also seemingly intended to be the final version. However, for reasons still unknown, the steps were filled in with local stone and the entire structure was then covered with a smooth facing of Tura limestone. The step pyramid was thus transformed into a geometrically true pyramid.

The superstructure, now visible, shows parts of the Third and Fourth steps of the seven-step stage, and all of the Fifth and Sixth steps of the Eight-step stage. Substantial parts of the lower portion of the ultimate pyramid at Meidum still remain intact.

The northern face of the pyramid contains an entrance to a corridor which leads downward to a depth of 190 feet through substratum of rock, levels off for 31 feet; then a vertical shaft leads upward into the burial chamber. No trace of a sarcophagus was found in 1882 when the chamber was first entered. It is thought that it was stolen in ancient times by robbers who dug a hole in the southern wall of the chamber.

The pyramid at Meidum had subsidiary buildings within an

enclosure. These consisted of a smaller pyramid, a mortuary temple and a third building. All these buildings have been reduced to nothing more than a pile of stones and try though Egyptologists will, little if any information can be ascertained from them.

No contemporary inscriptions have been found giving a possible hint as to the builder or the king to whom the pyramid at Meidum belongs. However, an inscription on the walls of the mortuary temple gives a possible clue: in the Eighteenth Dynasty, 1000 years later, or so, it was considered the work of Seneferu. Egyptologists are plagued by the difficulties of ascertaining with some degree of accuracy, who built the pyramids for whom. Without actual written evidence, all they have to go on is the estimation of the date the pyramid was built. Then they can only ascribe to the Pharaoh reigning at that particular time period. It has been conjectured that one Pharaoh may have been responsible for several pyramids but this has been objected to by Egyptologists who claim that this would be illogical. Nevertheless, records have been found referring to several pyramids of Seneferu. The possibility is very strong that not only was the pyramid at Meidum built for King Seneferu, but also two other pyramids 28 miles north of Meidum at Dahshur, one of them known as the Bent Pyramid.

The Bent Pyramid

The Bent Pyramid, also known as False, Rhomboidal and Blunted, lies to the south of the second of the group, and has definitely been ascribed to Seneferu. This pyramid appears to have been originally planned as a geometrically true pyramid but, for some unknown reason, was so hurriedly completed that the builders, in their haste, stopped before reaching the originally planned height. This deduction has been made because at about half-way up the pyramid, the angle of inclination decreases from roughly 54 degrees, 31 minutes to 43 degrees, 21 minutes. It has also been noted that it is not too accurately aligned to the cardinal points. Built on a base approximately 620 feet square, the Bent Pyramid would have reached a height of about 336 feet. Externally, it is the best preserved of all the existing pyramids. No other pyramid has retained so much of its outer casing. Internally, it is quite unique in that it has two separate entrances, one in the north face and another in the west face. The northern entrance leads downwards a distance of over 241 feet directly into an antechamber/vestibule, 16 feet wide and over 41 feet high. Directly beyond the ante-

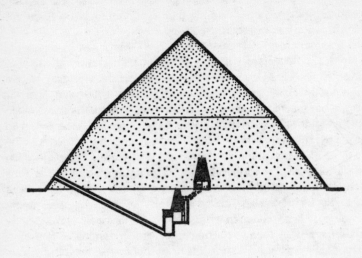

Figure 5. Plan of Bent Pyramid.

chamber/corridor is a second chamber about 16 by 20 feet and about 57 feet high. The second entrance in the west face, leads downwards nearly 211 feet, levels out for over 66 feet more and ends directly in the second chamber.

Not many objects were found in the chambers and corridors; some remains of an owl and several skeletons of bats were discovered wrapped together and in a wooden box in one of the floor cavities of the upper chamber. Here also, after considerable excavation of the two chambers, no sarcophagus was to be found, much to the dismay of the explorers.

The subsidiary pyramid, over 120 feet to the south, is 181 feet square and when finished must have measured over 106 feet high. This, too, has an entrance on the north face, which has a corridor descending into a small chapel with a pit in the middle of the floor. Directly beyond the chapel is a chamber nearly 8 feet square.

Subsidiary pyramids such as these are commonly found in the complexes of the main pyramids and are generally thought to have been used for one of two purposes: either they could have been the

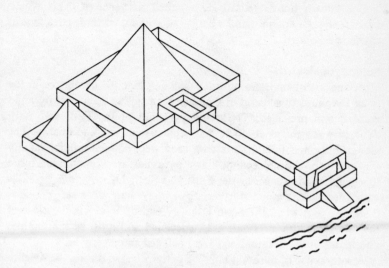

Figure 6. Typical Pyramid Complex.

Queen's Pyramids or they could have served as burial pyramids for the entrails of the kings.

The pyramid of Meidum provides the general plan for all the successive pyramidal complexes. It, like its successors, contained a main pyramid, a chapel, a smaller pyramid, and a mortuary temple, all enclosed within a wall. A causeway leading from the entrance of the mortuary temple connected to a valley temple on the bank of the Nile. This valley temple was built for the express purpose of receiving the body of the dead pharaoh, which was brought to it by boat. If the river had overflowed, the boat could dock directly at the temple; however, a canal was also dug, connecting the river to the door of the temple, so that in dry seasons the boat could still reach its mooring even if the river bank had receded from the temple entrance (see Fig. 6).

To the north of the Bent Pyramid stands a pyramid, known as the Northern Stone Pyramid of Dahshur. Strangely, this pyramid is nearly of the same angle of slope as the top half of the Bent Pyramid, 43 degrees and 36 minutes, and is 719 feet square at the base. The northern entrance leads down a corridor to twin ante-chambers and a main chamber over 50 feet high. The actual ownership of this pyramid is not known but is tentatively credited to Seneferu. This would indicate that he possibly had a choice of as many as three pyramids in which to be buried.

Later Pyramids

Once the art of majestic pyramid building reached its apogee in the Giza Pyramids (discussed in Chapter 5), a steady decline of pyramid construction prevailed. The many pyramids of the Fifth and Sixth dynasty were not as complex and grandiose in size and quality. The stones and other building material used were of such inferior quality that many of the succeeding kings' pyramids are now nothing more than rubble. However, in the Fifth and Sixth Dynasty artistic skills were developed much further than they had been in previous dynasties. But when the Sixth Dynasty ended, heralding the close of the Old Kingdom, arts and crafts declined and most of the temples and tombs of the Pyramid Age were pillaged and destroyed.

A resurgence of pyramid building activity began during the Twelfth Dynasty – the pyramids built being more ornate, but of lesser quality than the previous ones. Since the first Step Pyramid built in the Third Dynasty to the last major pyramid built in the Thirteenth Dynasty, only thirty pyramids are considered by Egyptologists to be of any consequence, either historically or architecturally (see list of pyramids on pages 00-0).

The absence of mummies in these, remains an inexplicable phenomena if one believes, as do most Egyptologists, that approximately one thousand years of pyramid building and elaborate tunnelling was performed for the sole purpose of the interment of the bodies of the pharaohs in sarcophagi. Obviously, the sealing of the sarcophagi and the many tunnels and passageways to 'safeguard the tomb from despoilers' becomes somewhat incomprehensible when, upon opening the burial chamber for the first time since it was sealed, no body is found. There are also cases where burial chambers were found with holes dug through one side. Egyptologists believe that these holes were dug by pillagers. If so, the robbers must have had great skill in tunnelling, a plan of the chambers within the pyramid and an insatiable desire not only for the precious jewels and other items entombed with the body, but also for the body itself!

Currently there are three major schools of thought on this subject.

Major Pyramids of Egypt*

Dynasty	Pharaoh	Base Dimensions	Location
3rd	Zoser	411 by 358 feet	Saqqara
3rd	Sekhemkhet	395 feet square	Saqqara
3rd	Khaba	276 feet square	Zawiyet el-Aryan
4th	Seneferu	473 feet square	Meidum
4th	Seneferu (bent)	620 feet square	Dahshur
4th	Seneferu	719 feet square	Dahshur
4th	Cheops (great)	756 feet square	Giza
4th	Djedefre	320 feet square	Abu Roash
4th	Chephren	708 feet square	Giza
4th	Mycerinus	356 feet square	Giza
5th	Userkaf	247 feet square	Saqqara
5th	Sahure	257 feet square	Abu Sir
5th	Neferirkare	360 feet square	Abu Sir
5th	Niuserre	274 feet square	Abu Sir
5th	Isesi	265 feet square	Saqqara
5th	Unas	220 feet square	Saqqara
6th	Teti	210 feet square	Saqqara
6th	Pepi I	250 feet square	Saqqara
6th	Merenre	263 feet square	Saqqara
6th	Pepi II	258 feet square	Saqqara
8th	Ibi	102 feet square	Saqqara
11th	Neb-hepet-Re Mentuhotep	70 feet square	Deir el-Bahri
12th	Ammenemes I	296 feet square	Lisht
12th	Sesostris I	352 feet square	Lisht
12th	Ammenemes II	263 feet square	Dahshur
12th	Sesostris II	347 feet square	Illahum
12th	Sesostris III	350 feet square	Dahshur
12th	Ammenemes III	342 feet square	Dahshur
12th	Ammenemes III	334 feet square	Hawara
13th	Khendjer	170 feet square	Saqqara

* According to I.E.S. Edwards in *The Pyramids of Egypt.*

The first claims that the tomb robbers took the bodies in order to completely defile the previous pharaoh. They disposed of the mummies in some unexplained way so that they are lost forever to posterity.

The second school believes that those burial chambers are actually dummy rooms and the real burial vaults are yet to be found within each pyramid. This explanation is more reasonable, since it is obvious

that even the immense pyramids, with all of their elaborate safe-
guards were vulnerable to thieves. Possibly the builders were cunning
enough to equip rooms with sealed sarcophagi and some jewels in
order to deceive thieves into believing they had actually found the
main chambers. This would explain the appearance of the alleged
burial chambers upon initial entry by modern archaeologists — empty
rooms devoid of everything save for sealed, yet empty, sarcophagi. It
is certainly conceivable that the pharaohs were extremely aware of the
skill and determination of the criminals of their days and in their
apparently successful efforts to confound them unwittingly created a
mystery which has endured to the present time.

The third group of scholars believes that the pyramids, especially
the Great Pyramid at Giza (see Chapters 6 & 7), were never built as
burial vaults but, instead, were created as temples of initiation. These
scholars have no theory as to why the sarcophagi have consistently
been found sealed but empty.

As has been seen, the mysteries of the pyramids are manifold —
even the experts cannot agree as to the real reason for the erection of
the pyramids, the methods of construction used in these massive
structures and, of course, the absence of mummies in what were,
apparently, sealed sarcophagi.

5

The Pyramids of Giza

Of all the Seven Wonders of the World, only the Great Pyramid of Giza remains today. Like the other pyramids of Egypt (discussed in the previous chapter), the Great Pyramid continues to confound Egyptologists, who are at a loss to explain the method and purpose of its construction.

Only a short camel ride from the modern city of Cairo, this ancient wonder stands, the *pièce de résistance* in a complex of structures consisting of three magnificent pyramids, a colossal sphynx, several lesser pyramids and a few tombs.

The largest pyramid is referred to as the Great Pyramid or the Pyramid of Cheops, Cheops being the Greek form of Khufu, the name of the Pharaoh who was the son and successor of Seneferu's throne. The Great Pyramid has become the apogee of pyramid building with respect to size and quality. Scores of attempts have been made to illustrate its size by comparing it with other famous structures. Originally it is thought to have been 481.4 feet high; the centuries have eroded it to its present height of 450 feet. It covers 13.1 acres and its side measurements, according to I.E.S. Edwards in *The Pyramids of Egypt*, at the base, have been surveyed as follows: east, 755.88 feet; west, 755.77 feet; north, 755.43 feet; south, 756.08 feet. Although no two sides are absolutely identical in length, the difference between the shortest and longest side is only 7.9 inches. Its four triangular faces incline at an angle of approximately 51 degrees, 52 minutes to the ground. The entire structure was originally oriented in line with true north and south.

One of the mysteries of the Great Pyramid at this point is that many archaeologists and explorers have surveyed it and obtained different measurements of its height. One source quotes it as 484 feet,

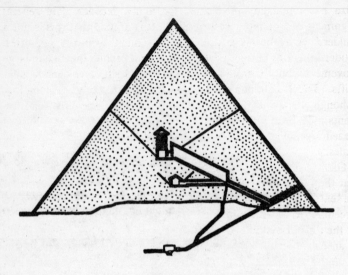

Figure 7. Plan of Great Pyramid.

another claims it to be 499 feet high. Some say its base is 756 feet square, others assert that it is 693 feet and that the triangular faces slope at an angle of 51 degrees, 19 minutes, 14 seconds. Presently its true north-south orientation contains the following estimated errors: northside – 2'28" south of west; southside – 1'57" south of west; eastside – 5'30" west of north; westside – 2'30" west of north. The accuracy of this orientation implies that the four corners were almost perfect right angles with their exact measurements being: northwest 89° 59'58"; northeast 90° 3'2"; southwest 90° 0'33"; southeast 89° 56'27".

This mystery of the orientation of the Great Pyramid of Giza is still unexplained. The most recent theory is that this is not a builder's error but is actually caused by continental drift. The following reprinted article by G.S. Pawley and N. Abrahamsen explains that although somewhat implausible, the Pyramids do show continental drift:

DO THE PYRAMIDS SHOW CONTINENTAL DRIFT?*

Abstract. The mystery of the orientation of the Great Pyramids of Giza has remained unexplained for many decades. The general alignment is 4 minutes west of north. It is argued that this is not a builders' error but is caused by movement over the centuries. Modern theories of continental drift do not predict quite such large movements, but other causes of polar wandering give even smaller shifts. Thus, continental drift is the most likely explanation, although somewhat implausible, especially as relevant measurements have been made over a 50-year period, whereas geophysical measurements of sea-floor spreading relate to million-year time scales.

Giza is situated approximately 30°E, 30°N; hence, we can say that the pole of about 4500 years ago (as seen from the centre of the earth) is now $3.5' \pm 0.9'$ along longitude 60°W toward Greenland, and with an unknown component along longitude 30°E. At the time of building, the 'pole star' would have been Vega. Being at an elevation of 30°, Vega would be ideal for alignment, but it would be worthwhile to conduct an experiment on the actual site so that all possible sources of error could be investigated.

It is now well documented that the true pole moves at 0.0032" annually along longitude 60°W (3). This would amount to 0.24' over 4500 years, which is far too small, and is of the wrong sign. Some variation is thought to be caused by the melting of the ice on Greenland and Antarctica. Other variations of the polar position are oscillatory in nature and are of very small amplitude (4).

Continental drift can cause the direction of true north to vary with respect to the moving block. The Americas have been separating from Africa and Europe owing to the spreading of the sea floor. This movement has a hinge southwest of Iceland, and is about 5cm per year between South America and Africa. If this causes only the latter to rotate and if the rotation is uniform, in 4500 years the pyramids would be rotated 0.1' in the observed sense.

Africa and the Arabian peninsula are moving apart as if hinged near the north end of the Red Sea. This suggests a rotation of the pyramids in the wrong sense, but again of a magnitude far too

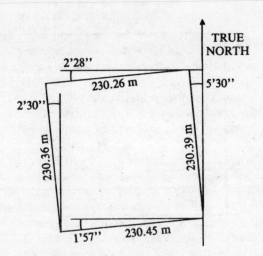

Figure 8(a). The Great Pyramids of Cheops.

small. Both these movements are shown in Figure 8(b).

Earthquakes are a possible mechanism for a local reorientation. The Mediterranean and Red Sea areas are well known for earthquakes, but a single quake of unprecedented magnitude would be needed to move the pyramids by strain release. Expert geological opinion would be worthwhile on this point as the local fault system must be understood in detail, as also the effect of the quake thought to have occurred in 908 B.C.

An observation of the movement of the pole exists on a time scale which is rare to modern science. The continental drift theory is based on very recent measurements, and there is controversy over whether drift is continuous or jerky. In this debate the pyramid observation may make a contribution, as it should be explainable in geophysical terms. Flinders Petrie (1) made the first (modern) detailed survey of the pyramids of Giza (2), but his observations seem to have been overlooked by scientists outside archaeology. He concluded that the average of some six alignments from the pyramids of Cheops (Khufu) — see Figure 8(a) — and

Figure 8(b). The pattern of Continental Drift, showing two hinge points.

Chephren (Khafra) was about 4′ west of true north, with an error of 1′. This indicated to him that the earth's pole had shifted by this amount.

Petrie argues that the east and west sides of each pyramid must have been set independently because the pyramids were built centred on a high point of bedrock. The entrance to Cheops' pyramid is in the form of a shaft with two distinct elevations, each section requiring independent alignment. As these are made of well-dressed and well-preserved rocks the alignments are still highly accurate, differing by only 1′. This is the origin of Petrie's estimate of alignment error, and it is well within the limits placed by the acuity of the eye which must have been used unaided by the builders.

An independent assessment of the builders' accuracy is afforded by the north and south sides of both pyramids. There is no direct astronomical method of east-west alignment, so that right angles must have been constructed. They were done with an accuracy of about 1.5′.

The northerly alignment must have been intended to be true north as there is no way of aligning to a point just off true north. A star so close to the pole would still describe a small circle in the sky, and this circle would alter considerably in its size in one generation owing to the precession of the equinoxes. Any thought of a magnetic alignment can be discarded because the magnetic variation over one generation would be enormous when the magnetic pole is near the true pole. In any case, the ancient Egyptians were not thought to have the lodestone, and this could never be used to achieve an accuracy of 1′. Petrie hints that astronomical parallax would have to be overcome by taking records 6 months apart, but it should be possible to get an alignment of the required accuracy in a single night.

There are no other remains in Egypt which can give corroborative results; the other pyramids are smaller and of less accuracy, and many other buildings have solar or stellar alignments. The two pyramids that give us this unique result were built at the zenith of pyramid construction, and it is not surprising that they alone yield such accuracy.

If we accept the evidence of the pyramids as valid we may well ask what other archaeological remains can give further information. There are some extremely accurate yet unexplained plateau markings in Peru, made by the Nazca people, and these are in danger of destruction. The megalithic sites in Britain and Brittany are also candidates for study, but first we must be convinced of the arguments that these are solar and lunar observatories (5). The best of these may be accurate enough, although this is doubtful. The pyramids probably yield the most accurate record, and it would be a pity if this unique fact was lost in the rush of science.

G.S. PAWLEY

Physics Department,
Edinburgh University,
Edinburgh, Scotland

N. ABRAHAMSEN

Laboratory of Geophysics, Aarhus
University, Aarhus, Denmark

References

1. F. Petrie, *Wisdom of the Egyptians* (Quaritch, London, 1940).
2. I.E.S. Edwards, *The Pyramids of Egypt* (Pelican, New Orleans, ed. 2, 1961).
3. W. Markowitz and B. Guinot, Eds., *Continental Drift* (Reidel, Dordrecht, Netherlands, 1968).
4. J. Coulomb and G. Jobert, *The Physical Constitution of the Earth* (Oliver and Boyd, Edinburgh, 1963).
5. A. Thom, *Megalithic Lunar Observations* (Oxford Univ. Press, New York, 1971).

When viewed from a distance the Great Pyramid gives the impression of being preserved substantially intact. However, when you get up close to it you see it has suffered greatly from the elements and by the hands of despoilers. A dozen or so courses and its capstone, which was possibly made of granite, have been removed from the apex. The entire facing of Tura limestone, with the exception of some pieces near the base, has been stripped from its triangular faces. The north face has a large opening cut into the core slightly below the original entrance. Moslem tradition relates that this aperture was made during the latter part of the ninth century in the mistaken belief that hidden treasures were contained within the pyramid. Subsequently, it became an abundant and convenient quarry for the provision stones required for bridges, walls, houses and other buildings in the neighbourhood of Giza and Cairo.

Modern science has unearthed still another mystery about the Great Pyramid; archaeologists have been unable to arrive at the exact computation of the amount of hewn stone in it. It is estimated, however, that when completed, the core of local stone and the outer facing of Tura limestone were composed of 2,300,000 separate blocks, each averaging $2\frac{1}{2}$ tons and reaching a maximum of 15 tons in weight. Other estimations range from 2 to 70 tons apiece, with the maximum number of blocks required in the Pyramid's construction reaching 2,500,000 pieces. It is thought that the centre of its core consists of a nucleus of rocks whose size cannot be precisely determined. No structure in the world which has been measured and surveyed as often and with as great as the Pyramid of Cheops has had such great discrepancies in the recording of its measurements. The only undisputed fact known about the pyramids is that the perfectly hewn granite and limestone blocks (to within 1/100 of an inch) were so accurately joined in the construction that the joints are never more than 1/50 of an inch wide.

The Interior of the Great Pyramid

Archaeologists consider the corridors and chambers of the Great Pyramid in relationship with its structural development. The entrance to the core of the Pyramid is in the north face, at a vertically measured height of 55 feet above ground level, and it is situated almost exactly midway across the face. From the entrance, a corridor little more than 3 feet square descends into an unfinished chamber at an angle slightly more than 26 degrees. A square pit is sunk into the trenched floor and the rough walls of the chamber contains an unfinished opening to a blind passage. The presence of this passage leads archaeologists to believe that if the original plan had been completed there would have been a second chamber beyond the first and interconnected with this blind corridor. When Herodotus visited Egypt during the middle of the Fifth Century B.C. he was told that beneath the Pyramid, vaults were constructed on a type of island which was surrounded by water channelled in from the Nile. On this island the body of Cheops was said to lie. However, no trace of this has yet been found and archaeologists think it unlikely that it ever existed. A somewhat more plausible alternative theory concerning the corridor and the unfinished chamber is that it was purposely left empty and unfinished to deliberately lead robbers to believe that no wealthy Pharaoh had been buried in the Pyramid. This is somewhat substantiated by another shaft leading to the descending corridor about 60 feet from the entrance of the unfinished chamber. This shaft could have served as a secondary maze to further confuse future plunderers. However, the most accepted theory is that this shaft was used as an air vent for the workers in the unfinished chamber.

Sixty feet into the descending corridor is the opening to the ascending corridor which corresponds in width and height to the descending corridor. The ascending corridor is approximately 129 feet in length, and its slope agrees with that of the descending corridor to within a fraction of a degree. Where the ascending corridor and the descending corridor meet, three large blocks made of granite and placed one behind another, plug the entrance into the ascending corridor from the descending corridor. These three granite plugs may possibly have had scores of limestone plugs behind them. Arab historians record that in the Ninth Century B.C. at the command of the Caliph Ma'mun, son of Harun al-Rashid, of *Arabian Nights* fame, the tunnellers redirected their digging when a slab of limestone, fashioned so that it was indistinguishable from the remainder of the roof near the upper end of the descending corridor, collapsed. During this retunnelling procedure they encountered three six-foot granite plugs beyond which was a passageway plugged with several limestone blocks. The peculiar fact about these plugs is that they would fit just as tightly the depth at the upper end of the passage as they did the lower end.

So great was the engineering agility and skill required to manoeuvre these granite blocks into place that how it was accomplished still remains a mystery. Even more mysterious, however, is where these blocks were stored prior to the burial of the pharaoh; or, if the blocks were placed before the interment took place, how the body was entombed with the plugs blocking the entranceway to the burial chamber. Many theories have been offered to explain these mysteries, all too implausible to be given serious consideration. To this day, the granite plugs remain in place, a mute testimonial to the genius of the Pharaoh's architect.

A chamber, built at the end of the passage from the top of the ascending corridor, and called by the Arabs 'the Queen's Chamber' is calculated to be exactly midpoint between the north and south sides of the Pyramid, and directly under the capstone. The Queen's Chamber shows indications that work was abandoned before completion. It measures more than 17 by 18 feet with a pointed roof rising to a height of over 20 feet. The east wall contains a niche $3\frac{1}{2}$ feet deep, 15 feet high and 5 feet wide, which was presumably designed to contain a statue which may never have been placed in position. The Queen's Chamber contains two shafts with a dead end, one on the north wall and the other on the south wall. Many researchers believe these shafts were once ventilating shafts much like the one for the unfinished chamber, but most probably were part of the maze system of tunnelling used to discourage despoilers from reaching the king's chamber. A third theory claims these shafts were for some astrological purpose used in the surveying process of building the Pyramid and chambers.

The continuation of the ascending corridor at the 129 foot mark is in the form of one of the Pyramid's most celebrated architectural works, 'The Grand Gallery'. It is over a hundred feet long and nearly

30 feet high. Both walls of polished limestone reach a height of $7\frac{1}{2}$ feet. At the foot of each wall a catwalk two feet high and $1\frac{3}{4}$ feet wide runs along the length of the Gallery with a passage $3\frac{1}{2}$ feet wide between the catwalks. The Gallery was constructed with a slope of 26 degrees and was so designed as to create a cumulative pressure all the way down the roof, causing each stone to be individually held up by the side wall. At the lower end of the Grand Gallery a gap now exists, caused by the removal of the stones which formerly linked the floor of the passage with the ascending corridor, and also covered the mouth of the horizontal passage leading to the Queen's Chamber. Removal of the lowest stone in the gap revealed a shaft which descends into the west wall of the descending corridor.

A stone raised three feet from the floor located at the upper end of the Grand Gallery gives access to a narrow, low passageway less than four feet square leading to the King's Chamber. About a third of the way along this polished limestone passageway enlarges into a sort of antechamber of polished red granite. The passageway then continues at its original aperture of less than four feet square opening into the King's Chamber.

The King's Chamber is completely built of polished red granite blocks, measuring slightly over 17 by 34 feet wide and 19 feet high. In the north and south walls, there are shafts similar to the ones found in the Queen's Chamber and the unfinished chamber. These shafts apparently at one time penetrated the core of the Pyramid and reached the outer surface. Near the west wall a lid-less, rectangular granite sarcophagus stands. Egyptologists vehemently insist that this sarcophagus contained the king's body, which was probably enclosed within an inner coffin of wood. The mystery of the sarcophagus is that its width is 1 inch greater than the width of the ascending corridor. Because it could not have been brought through that corridor, archaeologists conclude that it must have been placed in position while the chamber was being built.

There appears to be no exact architectural parallel to the roof and flat ceiling of the King's Chamber. Its flat ceiling of nine limestone slabs weighs an approximate total of 400 tons. Three more ceilings of exact construction are separated by compartments; the fifth and final ceiling is pointed. It is thought the purpose of this particular construction of the roof was to eliminate any risk of the chamber's ceiling collapsing under the weight of the surrounding superstructure and the forces of nature. Their construction has been justified because every one of the massive slabs of granite in the ceiling including those in the relieving compartments are cracked, presumably by earth quakes, and yet none have collapsed.

It is thought that The Great Pyramid was first violated by plunderers during the beginning of the First Intermediate Period, somewhere within the Seventh Dynasty. Several other violations appear to have been perpetrated, and each time the Great Pyramid was renovated and the entrance concealed. These security measures were to cause archaeologists, centuries later, great difficulty in gaining entry to the Pyramid.

The Pyramids of Chephren and Mycerinus

The second pyramid at Giza is that of King Chephren (known to the Egyptians as *Khaef-Rē*). Chephren's pyramid actually appears taller than the Great Pyramid, simply because it is situated on slightly higher ground. Its measurements at the time of construction were nearly 708 feet square and 471 feet high; note it is slightly more than 690 feet square and reaches a height of only 448 feet. The other reason for the illusion of greater height is that although the base of Chephren's pyramid is smaller than that of Cheops', its faces slope at a steeper angle, 52 degrees, 20 minutes, which allowed it to reach a height of only 10 feet less than the Great Pyramid.

The exterior of Chephren's pyramid is somewhat unique in two respects: it is faced with two different types of stone, and most of its facing is still intact. The outer casing which remains intact near the apex is of Tura limestone, while the casing at the base is of red granite.

There are, surprisingly, two entrances to the substructure on the north side of the pyramid. One entrance is situated on the north face of the pyramid, and the other is directly beneath it, just past the foundation wall of the pyramid. Both corridors from each entrance descend at about the same angle. The upper corridor, lined with red granite, levels out and leads into a chamber $46\frac{1}{2}$ feet long, $16\frac{1}{2}$ feet wide and $22\frac{1}{2}$ feet high. Interestingly, the chamber is aligned with its shortest side in the north-south direction. The entire chamber, except for the roof was hewn out of the rock beneath the pyramid. The roof, which is within the pyramid structure itself, is gabled of slabs of limestone which were laid at the same angle as that of the faces of the pyramid. Signs of attempts to place ventilating shafts, similar to those in Cheops' pyramid, are apparent but were never undertaken. Near the west side of the chamber a magnificent polished granite rectangular sarcophagus is sunk into the floor up to the lid. The lid was found removed and broken in two when the chamber was first entered by archaeologists in 1818. Of course, no mummy was found.

The lower corridor levels out after its descent, much like the upper corridor, and then slopes upward again to enter the horizontal part of the upper chamber through its floor. The horizontal portion of the lower corridor contains an entrance ramp in the west side which leads into a chamber slightly larger than 34 feet long, 10 feet wide and 8 feet high. It is thought that this chamber was originally intended to be the tomb and for some reason the larger chamber was built to receive the sarcophagus.

The third pyramid in the group is ascribed to Mycerinus. However, there are no validated records available to shed light on the life and character of Mycerinus. The only structure even nearly completed among the pyramid complex of Mycerinus is the actual pyramid; the subsidiary buildings are in various stages of completion. The Pyramid of Mycerinus covers less than one-fourth of the area of Cheops' Pyramid and was originally 218 feet high. It now stands only 204 feet.

As on the facing of Chephren's Pyramid, the pyramid of Mycerinus has Tura limestone facing on the uppermost section and red granite casing on the lower section. The interior of the pyramid is not unique in its planning, and is somewhat similar to that of the Great Pyramid. There is evidence of a corridor, thought to be originally the primary entrance to the pyramid, which was never finished; a second, lower corridor was built instead. The possibility exists that this blind corridor may perhaps have been intended to lead to another chamber, the construction of which was never even begun because of the untimely death of Mycerinus.

The entrance corridor leads into an ante-chamber and then continues into a large rectangular room, whose longest axis is aligned east-west. At the end of this room is what is thought to be the burial chamber. This is built entirely of granite − walls, floor and pointed roof. The underside of the roof was rounded to give a barrel-vault effect.

The British colonel Howard Vyse originally opened the pyramid of Mycerinus during his excavations of 1837 and 1838. He found a sealed rectangular, panel-decorated, carved basalt sarcophagus; also, some human bones and the lid of a wooden coffin inscribed with the name of Mycerinus. Colonel Vyse decided to ship the presumably never-opened sarcophagus back to England. Unfortunately, the ship floundered off the coast of Spain and the sarcophagus was lost. This sinking led to the story of the fulfilment of a so-called mummy's curse which periodically makes a sensational story for the news media. There is no known record of whether the sarcophagus was empty or not. It has been difficult to identify the owners of the many subsidiary pyramids and mini-pyramids in each of the three pyramid complexes. The builders are assumed to be those of the original main pyramids. The difficulty lies in the fact that after the pyramid complexes were built, many noblepeople and others of even lesser rank had themselves buried in vaults, chambers and mini-pyramids either within or close to the complex, in order that they might receive the benefit of being buried near their idols and perhaps reap the same benefits in the after-life and live with their pharaohs.

The Sphinx

It is thought that during the time of Chephren, the Sphinx was carved from a monolith left as surplus by the builders of the Great Pyramid. The Sphinx is, as most authorities agree, a recumbent lion with a human head. When completed, it probably had a covering of plaster and was painted with royal colours. The symbol of royalty is well portrayed by the beard on its chin, the cobra snake on its forehead and the royal headdress. The width of the face alone, is nearly 14 feet at its maximum. The colossal figure is over 66 feet high and more than 240 feet long; its weight is estimated to be in hundreds, if not thousands, of tons.

Although now very much in disrepair, it is believed that the human face was either originally intended to be that of Chephren, or perhaps was revamped during his reign to resemble him.

The dream of Tuthmosis IV of the Eighteenth Dynasty is recorded on a red granite stone which is perched between the paws of the Sphinx. The stone's story has been deciphered to explain that one day, when Tuthmosis was still a prince, he decided to rest during a hunting expedition. He fell asleep in the shade of the Sphinx, and had a dream in which the Sphinx, regarded at that time to be the sun god Harmachis, promised to reward him with the double crown of Egypt if he were to clear the sand away from the Sphinx and restore its majestic beauty. The rest of the inscription is too worn to relate just how the promise was fulfiled. Apparently it was, because Tuthmosis IV did have the Sphinx restored.

The mythology of the Egyptians always contains a lion as the

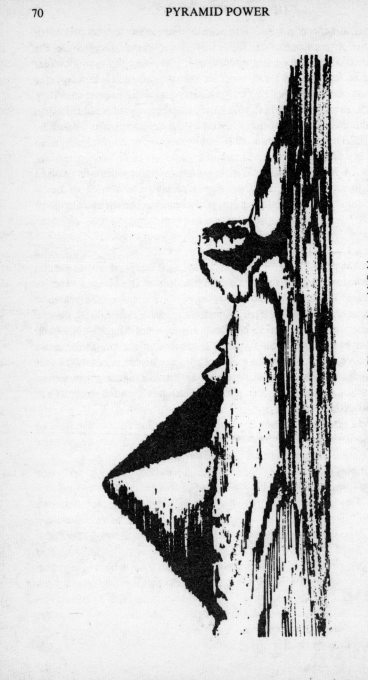

Figure 9. Sketch of Giza complex with Sphinx.

guardian of sacred places. This could date back to the priests of Heliopolis who incorporated into their solar creed, the lion as the guardian of the gates of the underworld. The lion, as symbolized by the Sphinx, retained the function of a sentinel, while its human features are thought to have been those of an early sun deity known as Atum. When the face of the Sphinx was re-chiselled to resemble Chephren's, it is probable that the pharaoh identified with the sun god and intended that the Sphinx represent him (Chephren) as the solar deity in its sentinel position by the Giza Pyramids.

There are some experts who believe that there may be some tunnels or corridors to which access is gained through a hidden entrance on the structure of the Sphinx, linking the three main pyramids to their secret burial chambers. However, no such secret passageway has been found, and the accepted premise is that it does not exist.

Colossal pyramids; missing mummies; scant pieces of jewellry and furniture, apparently left as token items for robbers of burial vaults; missing capstones; empty sarcophagi; mind-boggling feats of engineering: these are the clues, scattered over a mere 500 years, to what is perhaps the most perplexing mystery of all time. And, to add to the intrigue, it appears from the records surviving from the Old Kingdom Period that the peoples of successive Egyptian dynasties were as mystified by it all as we are today.

In the next chapter, we will discuss the theories of the purpose and construction methods of the pyramids, as propounded by modern Egyptologists.

6

From Foundation to Capstone: The How and Why of Pyramid Construction

Existing records throw little light upon the lives, habits and customs of the pharaol s of the Old Kingdom. And virtually nothing is known about the method of construction of the pyramids and lesser subsidiary buildings within each pyramid complex of that period.

Egyptologists can only make educated guesses about the construction methods employed by the pyramid builders. Close scrutiny of each building and of the available tools, combined with assumptions of practicability and present expert knowledge of masonry have led archaeologists to develop theories about pyramid, and general, building construction. Unfortunately, these theories are now accepted as fact, even though there is no irrefutable proof that any of the massive structures built in the Old Kingdom, or before, were actually erected in the manner that the Egyptologists claim they were.

Choice of the West Bank
Most of the pyramids were built on the west bank of the Nile, on high ground so that the complex would not be flooded when the Nile rose, and yet close enough so that the workers could have access to the river, on which were shipped the building stones from the quarries. Presently, the inundations of the Nile bring the pyramids at Dahshur about a mile from the river's bank, while the Giza pyramids are only one-quarter mile away, and the pyramid at Meidum is only three city blocks from the river's edge.

Another seemingly apparent reason for the choice of the west bank as the construction site is that the underlying rock foundation of the chosen site had to be solid, with no faults, or else the entire complex would have collapsed, perhaps even while under construction. The Egyptians must have been the world's best geologists, far superior to those of today, since they were able to determine that the west bank of the Nile was the correct site for the pyramid complex. The amount of technical expertise required to determine that the huge area had a solid rock foundation is immense, and requires fantastically extensive knowledge in the many fields associated with proper geological surveying.

It is reasoned by the Egyptologists that the ancient Egyptians constructed the pyramid complex on the west bank of the Nile because they wanted to be as close as possible to the setting sun. Since the setting of the sun symbolized death, this reasoning strikes us as a bit far-fetched — if they had positioned the pyramids for symbolic significance, it would have made more sense for them to build them on the *east bank* (symbolizing birth) so that their pharaohs would be closer to rebirth and so that they themselves could be close to the birth or rebirth of their gods.

We can only conclude that the Egyptians chose the pyramid sites not for symbolic reasons but for practical ones.

Clearing and Preparation of the Site

Having determined the construction site, the builders then had to clear hundreds if not thousands of acres of sand and stone from the surface covering the solid rock foundation. The foundation itself then had to be levelled and smoothed. The levelling was so exact that the Great Pyramid is out of level by less than half an inch. Over the course of 765 feet, one-half inch deviation is, by any reckoning, negligible. One-half inch equals 1/24 feet, or approximately 0.05 feet. This means an error of only 0.05/750 or 0.007 percent. Such a slight deviation from accuracy rivals inaccuracies existing in most edifices constructed today.

It is believed that the site was cleared by the manual labour of upwards of hundreds of thousands of people, and the levelling was accomplished by cutting trenches into the natural rock foundation, filling these trenches with water and damming them up. The foundation was then honed down until it was level with the water. The trenches were then undammed and filled in with solid stone.

The next stage was to survey the area in order to insure that the base would be perfectly square, and that each side would be in line with each cardinal point. To align the building along either the north-south axis or the east-west axis would actually require the surveyors to locate only one side; the remaining three sides would then automatically be positioned correctly. Several aspects of this alignment must be assumed, because there is no surviving evidence of instruments used for this purpose. In fact, it appears that even the compass was unknown at that time.

Seemingly, Egyptian knowledge of astronomy was beyond the limits of the science practised by the members of the civilization of the day. Consequently, modern astronomers are at a loss to explain the manner in which these ancients arrived at some of their astronomical interpretations. The set-square and the plumb-bob are only assumed to have existed. These two instruments are primary to the construction of buildings in that they insure that the corners are square to each other and that the walls are straight or angled properly to form the desired slope.

Quarrying and Transporting the Stone

While the construction site was being prepared, quarriers working at Tura, on the east bank of the Nile in the Muqattam hills, were quarrying the limestone block necessary for the pyramids. Up the Nile, near Aswan, quarriers were acquiring the granite blocks needed for the edifice. The method of quarrying these tremendous blocks of stone can only be inferred from some existing tools discovered by archaeologists. These Egyptians claim that the quarriers dug, chiselled, hacked, wedged and pounded to split the huge blocks out of tunnels dug deep into rock beds, and then scraped, polished and finished these monoliths into nearly perfect cubes. This, they allege, was done with copper tools tempered by highly skilled smiths in order to impart the strength required to shape stone. However, none of the highly tempered tools have even been found and it seems impossible for any smith to hone and temper copper to such a degree that it is capable of cutting stone. This is particularly hard to accept in light of the fact that people today have great difficulty in maintaining the sharpness of the finest and most expensive cutlery used for nothing stronger than cutting meat, produce and fabric. Even alloys of extreme durability and highest quality offer limited longevity for oil well drillers; these tremendously expensive cutters require frequent sharpening and maintenance before their usefulness expires.

After quarrying the blocks, the next remarkable achievement was to transport them to the building site. The quarriers at one site actually had to ship the stones upstream, while the other quarriers had the simpler task of sending them downstream. This, the experts claim, was only done during the time that the Nile was overflowing, because the shippers would then be afforded the greatest possibility of arriving close to the building site. However, this would actually have created an additional problem for the shippers since, when any river is over-flowing, the current has such tremendous force that it is virtually impossible to navigate on the water.

Another massive problem with which the shippers had to cope was the designing of boats or barges which would buoy weights so great they stagger the imagination: the blocks of quarried stone averaged $2\frac{1}{2}$ tons, while some subsidary buildings required stone blocks of over 200 tons. The barges would have had to have been extremely large to handle such weight. None of these barges (nor any remnants of them) have ever been found, nor does any record of them exist.

The shippers were also faced with the task of loading and un-loading the barges. What extensive equipment these people must have had in order to lift a 200 ton monolith and balance it on a barge so perfectly that it would not capsize the vessel. They were then required to unload their massive cargo at the building site. The banks were very treacherous during the time of inundation because of the many shifting sand banks. Therefore, even though the barges were able to be navigated close to the building site, there had to be very long-armed beams to hoist the 200 ton blocks off the barge and onto hard-packed sand. The dock area would still have been dozens of feet away from the actual unloading and depot site. It seems reasonable to assume that very firm sand, with a substrata of rock was necessary to support the tonnage of blocks, plus the cranes and auxiliary equipment necessary for unloading procedure. The engineering feats performed by the Egyptians in transporting and unloading the stones rivals those performed today with the use of the modern techniques and equipment of our experts. This became evident in the 1960s when the Aswan Dam was nearing completion. A united effort was made by many engineers, using sophisticated equipment from all over the world, to save as many temples, palaces and statues as possible before the Aswan damming would inundate these colossal masterpieces forever. But all the modern equipment and expertise of the highly trained and skilled engineers could not lift many of the single monoliths. The stones actually had to be broken into smaller pieces in order to make the relocation attempt a reality. Because the experts needed to cut up the blocks of stone, which the Egyptians obviously had been able to handle intact, a very small percentage of the actual targeted edifices could be saved from the inundating waters of the Aswan Dam.

However difficult it was for the shippers to manage the transport of the blocks on the river, they must have been even more troubled by the task of transporting the stones over land that was not every solid. It is possible that wheeled vehicles were used – a picture in the Fifth Dynasty tomb of Kaemheset at Saqqara depicts a wheeled scaling-ladder. But there is no evidence to support the wheeled-vehicle theory. Paintings on tomb walls from the Eighteenth Dynasty period depict men transporting statues and heavy bricks by pulling sledges with ropes along a wood-paved way. It is believed that water or oil was poured under the sledge to reduce the friction. This explanation of how the stones were transported actually raises more questions than it settles. For one thing, timber in that area was very scarce – all that was available was palm trees and the Egyptians, to whom these date-producing trees were essential for food, would not have been likely to cut them down for paving roads. If the lumber for the roadways was imported, and there is no record that this kind of importation took place until over a thousand years after the pyramids were built, what kind of lumber was it and from where was it imported? Another flaw in the wooden road theory is that even if the sandy soil was paved over with timber in order to create a fairly level and smooth surface over which the monoliths could be dragged, the timbers would repeatedly have had to be replaced because they would have eventually splintered from the dynamic pressure of such enormous weight being constantly dragged over them. Such a replacement procedure would have been exorbitantly time-consuming and costly.

Possible Methods of Construction

The questions raised above – of how the blocks were quarried and transported, and of how the sites were cleared and levelled – pale beside the mystery which is today creating the greatest controversy among Egyptologists: how were the builders able to maintain the internal and external regularities of the form of the pyramid. Many theories have emerged concerning the actual construction method of the Great Pyramid, but no evidence to support any of them has ever been uncovered during archaeological excavations.

So great is the controversy over this question that in 1970 *Natural*

History, the journal of the American Museum of Natural History, devoted space in their November and December issues (volume 79, numbers 9 and 10) to a debate between several Egyptologists over the possible construction methods used to build the Great Pyramid of Egypt.

One of these Egyptologists, Olaf Tellefsen, claims that the Egyptians did not use a ramp and sledge to construct the Pyramid, and that it required only about 3000 construction workers to raise the Pyramid. Engineer Tellefsen bases his argument on his observation of three men moving large stones to the edge of the river Nile. The men were using a primitive piece of engineering equipment – a long weight arm. The weight arm was about 18 feet long and was pivoted at the 3 foot point by a fulcrum about 6 feet high. The longer arm had a platform attached to it, upon which rocks were placed at counter-weight. Rocks would then be piled on to the platform until they would begin to lift the estimated 2 ton stone. Then the men had no difficulty in swinging and applying their own force to the arm until the block of stone was in proper position over rollers. The counterweight of rocks was then removed until the stone block settled onto the rollers and the remaining rocks were then dumped. Two of the men then began to push the block of stone with wooden levers while the third shifted the rollers. Tellefsen concluded that he had witnessed an engineering feat which the three men had inherited from the past. From this he envisioned an entire pyramid complex built using the level arm principle in the same way as those three men had. He further envisioned adaptation of the lever arm principle that would have moved stone blocks laterally as well as vertically. Tellefsen does not discuss the quarrying, dressing or transportation of the blocks of stone, nor does he mention the length of time his conception of the Pyramid construction would have taken the Egyptians. He simply attempts to explain from a fresh point of view, the possible engineering process employed in building the Pyramid and claims that Herodotus' description of how the Egyptians built the pyramid actually applies only to the final casing stones and not to the entire structure.

Kent Weeks and I.E.S. Edwards, two noted Egyptologists, take strong exception to Olaf Tellefsen's theory and cling to the ramp and sledge explanation.

According to Weeks, there is considerable evidence favouring the use of ramps and sledges to build pyramids. He bases this contention on the tomb paintings of the Eighteenth Dynasty depicting a ramp

used in the erection of columns in a temple courtyard, and the
discovery of the remains of ramps at several dig sites, including Giza.
These ramps, found near pyramids, had a slope of about 15 degrees,
which Weeks claims is 'an eminently manageable angle up which to
pull blocks'. He also cites an Old Kingdom record stating that 3000
men were required to haul a sarcophagus lid from the quarry to the
Nile. It is estimated that there was a population of approximately 1.5
to 2 million during the Old Kingdom period. Weeks suggests that the
claims of Herodotus that over 400,000 people were involved in
building the Pyramid were somewhat exaggerated since this would
mean that about one-third of the existing population was employed in
pyramid building. Instead, Weeks believes that an estimated figure of
100,000 men is more realistic.

The most conservative of the three, I.E.S. Edwards, clings to the
theories propounded by earlier Egyptologists. He states that since
these theories are based on actual archaeological finds, it is pointless
to dispute them unless or until new archaeological evidence is
uncovered which would compel revision of traditional thinking on the
subject.

Edwards also states that there is no evidence as to the exact size of
the population at the time of the building of the Great Pyramid and
there is not even enough information available to afford speculation in
this area. He also claims that to refer to the writings of Herodotus is
not relevant because it 'is not equal to citing contemporary evidence'.

It seems to us that we must, at least in part, agree with Olaf
Tellefsen's suggestion that Egyptologists cling over-tenaciously to the
ramp and sledge theory. The arguments which they offer in evidence
are certainly debatable and do not warrant the acceptance they have
received – acceptance to the point where many people actually believe
that it is an indisputable fact that the ramp method was used by the
Egyptians in building the pyramids. Actually, there is no solid
evidence to support anything the Egyptologists have said or written
about the pyramids of any dynasty, or about the pharaohs and their
civilizations.

We have now come to believe that all of the writings on Egyptian
history are nothing more than theory and are not based on any
evidence contemporary to the period under consideration. In other
words, pictures of pyramid building or statue transportation on the
walls of Eighteenth Dynasty tombs are *not* contemporary to the
Fourth Dynasty any more than stainless steel statues of twentieth

century buildings would be considered contemporary to the twelfth century. That ramps were discovered near pyramids does not prove that the ramps were used to build all the pyramids on the site – if some of the pyramids were built in the Fourth Dynasty and others in the Eighteenth, it is possible that the ramps were used only in the construction of the later dynasty pyramids. Another possibility is that the ramps were actually used in the *dismantling* of the outer casing stones, which were then used in another construction.

It is very important to remember that many archaeological sites contain relics of several thousands of years. Especially in the light of the discovery that Carbon 14 dating is not too reliable, it seems rather irresponsible to unequivocally attribute a particular artifact to a particular age or dynasty. It cannot be too strongly stressed that there is absolutely no evidence contemporary to the building of the great Pyramids which proves that the ramp and sledge method was employed by its builders. The artifacts of later ages can only be accepted as contemporary to those ages and one can do no more than speculate as to whether or not they were also employed in earlier times.

It is interesting to note that while archaeologists are apparently relatively content to ascribe the building practices of the Eighteenth Dynasty to those of the first five dynasties, these same authorities point out that the pyramids of the later pharaohs are obviously inferior, in terms of craftsmanship and technical expertise, to the pyramids of the Old Kingdom. Oddly enough, these Egyptologists see no inconsistency in their attribution of identical building techniques to structures which differ widely in the quality of their construction.

Some Unsolved Mysteries

There are a number of other unsolved mysteries which arise in connection with the actual construction of the Great Pyramid. One of these concerns the materials used on the outer surfaces of the pyramids of the Old Kingdom. This controversy has arisen because of a hieroglyphic sign which appears on the wall of each burial chamber in every pyramid of the Old Kingdom period. This sign represents a pyramid in white, with a black base, reddish brown speckled sides and a capstone of blue or yellow. Some Egyptologists interpret this hieroglyph to mean that the outer surface of the finished pyramid was painted, perhaps after the application of plaster to give the surface a smooth finish. Others believe that the white part of the hieroglyph represents the naturally white Tura limestone. They further speculate that, contrary to accepted belief, another type of stone, one with a speckled appearance, was actually used on the sides and that only the base and capstone were painted.

The only known records on the subject of the building of the Great Pyramid are writings of the Greek historian Herodotus, who visited Egypt during the Fifth Century B.C., around the time of the Twenty-eighth Dynasty, at least two thousand years after the erection of the monumental structure. According to the historian, the Great Pyramid was built in twenty years by 400,000 labourers. These labourers were divided into four groups of 100,000 men each. Each group worked on the construction of the pyramid for a period of four months per year. If we accept this number as correct — and there is no source other than Herodotus to which one can turn for that information — we must then conclude that the Egyptian officials were faced with the interesting problem of providing food, shelter, sanitation facilities etc., for 100,000 workers. Even if there were only 200,000 men in total, each working for a period of six months, the same problem would have existed. Yet there is no evidence of any structures or facilities which might have been used to house such a massive number of workers. The alternative, then, is that the construction workers did not actually live at the site but commuted to it daily from their homes. Since the only modes of transportation were via foot, waterway or animal-back, it is obvious that commuting was hardly as speedy as it is today. A reasonable estimate of the time it would have taken a worker to arrive at the construction site from his home is three hours. Given six hours of travel time per day, and a probable ten or twelve hour work schedule, the pyramid construction builder was left with a maximum of eight hours of sleeping time (skipping meals and any other activity) in which to recuperate from what must have been excruciatingly exhausting work.

Still another dispute centering around the construction workers themselves is the contention of some authorities that the workers were executed after the pyramid on which they were working was built so that they would not be able to reveal the secret of the passageways leading to the burial chamber. If this were the case, mass graves would have been required. So far, none have been found. Of course, other methods, such as the use of gigantic funeral pyres, could have been employed to dispose of the bodies. However, no records or evidence exists to confirm such a supposition. But common sense suggests that such mass executions would have been, to say the least, impractical, since they would have wiped out the major portion of the Egyptian population, not to mention a sizeable percentage of the total world population. Having committed such a massive genocidal action, the pharaohs would then have had to wait for a minimum of fifteen or twenty years until the population had regenerated itself to the point where there were enough people to build a new pyramid. But, according to the archaeologists themselves, several pyramids were built within a few years of each other. These two beliefs then raise an interesting paradox: men who have just been executed cannot function as construction workers.

Another case in which the archaeologists have demonstrated their willingness to accept hearsay as fact is on the subject of the time it took to build a pyramid. Herodotus' claim that the building of the Great Pyramid took twenty years is, of course, totally unsupported. Further, he makes no statement whatsoever as to the length of time it took to build the lesser pyramids. Nevertheless, archaeologists have eagerly pounced on the twenty-year time period and have blithely assigned it to all pyramidal construction.

The purpose to which the pyramids were put apparently does not present as much of a problem to Egyptologists as does the construction. They are convinced that the pyramids were used as tombs to inter the bodies of the deceased pharaohs. The burial customs of upper and lower Egypt, before unification, were completely different. Upper Egyptians buried their dead in cemeteries situated near the edge of the desert. These graves were usually lined with brick, had timber roofs and were marked with a mound of sand. The burial of bodies in lower Egypt however, was actually done beneath the floor of one of the rooms of the house. This is what leads Egyptologists to believe that when the two parts of Egypt were unified, the burial custom of lower Egypt was adopted and from this there was a simple transition to full blown pyramidal burial houses. Another simple transition could have been achieved by using the pyramid as a great monument, marking the location of the grave instead of using sand as a mound marker. According to Egyptologists, the transition from the mound burial (or *mastaba* structure burial) to the step pyramid may be related to Incantation Number 267 of the Pyramid texts carved on walls of the chambers and corridors of pyramids in the late Fifth and early Sixth Dynasties. This incantation read: 'A staircase to heaven is laid for him (the pharaoh) so that he may mount up to heaven thereby.' Therefore it is assumed that the king thought he or, more probably, his spiritual body, could approach the celestial heaven via a staircase. It was then obviously necessary to construct a symbolic staircase. This could have been done in the form of a step pyramid.

One theory as to the reason for the evolution of the step pyramid into the true pyramid is that an Egyptian (and a member of a sun-worshipping race) one cloudy day drew a picture of four rays of sun shining through the clouds at such an angle as to form a pyramid. The drawing later served as the basis for the plan of a true pyramidal building. This rather ingenious explanation is not readily accepted by the majority of experts.

Interesting enough, this particular aspect of pyramid building does not seem to have caught the interest of Egyptologists and there are no other theories as to the motivation behind the construction of the first true pyramids.

It should be mentioned here that throughout the Middle East there was a prevailing philosophy which required the erection of tall buildings to bring worshippers closer to their gods. In Mesopotamia, for instance, tall brick towers called *ziggurats* were built precisely for this purpose. There are some people who believe that the Tower of Babel was actually a Babylonian ziggurat.

Speculation about the purposes of the pyramids is, of course, not unique to archaeologists and historians of the twentieth century. The Arabs associated the pyramids with scriptural accounts of the flood. They claimed that the pyramids were built as a result of a dream in which the dreamer was warned that a great flood would come and destroy all Egyptian wisdom and knowledge. Because dreams were regarded with great respect and awe, this warning was taken seriously and vaults, in the shape of pyramids, were built to preserve the precious records from the flooding.

Another speculation, which arose sometime before the Fifth Century A.D., was that the pyramids were the graneries in which Joseph stored the corn during the seven lean years. This belief survived through the Middle Ages and is still preserved in pictorial form in the decorated dome of the Church of St Mark in Venice, Italy.

In the 1850s, a man named John Taylor published his speculation that Cheops' pyramid was built by a race of non-Egyptians under the direction of God.

Today's prevailing theory is that the pyramids of Egypt were built as tombs. Egyptologists are firm and unshakably convinced of the validity of their belief in this assumption, despite the fact that archaeologists investigating virtually identical pyramids in South and Meso-America are equally firmly convinced that the American pyramids were built as temples.

We believe that present day theorists have allowed themselves to become so preoccupied with their own theories, and are so busy defending any challenges to them, that they are unable to deal with other hypotheses which might very well be as sound as their own.

It seems to us that so long as Egyptologists continue to squabble over the methods of construction used to build the Great Pyramid, with the members of each school of thought tenaciously and blindly clinging to their own theories, like small children stubbornly hanging on to old, soiled teddy bears, the mystery, if there is one at all, will never be solved.

In the second part of this treatise we give serious consideration to the many currently accepted theories of why the Great Pyramid was built.

PART 2
TREASURE OF THE PAST, SOURCE FOR THE FUTURE: THE POWER OF THE PYRAMID

7

Pyramid Power

In any argument on the Great Pyramid at Giza, the only point on which archaeologists, Egyptologists, scientists and scholars agree is that it was built by Cheops somewhere between 2686 and 2181 B.C. As we discussed in the previous chapter, there is no irrefutable evidence of the time during which the pyramid was built, by whom it was built, or for what purpose – most people have now come to accept this assumption as fact.

The exceptions to the believers in the 'Cheops theory' are psychics, seers, sensitives and others usually classified as mystics or occultists. Many of these persons believe that the Pyramid is much older than 5000 years and was used for purposes other than a tomb.

The Theories of Edgar Cayce and Manley P. Hall

Edgar Cayce, the world's greatest psychic, said in one of his readings that the Pyramid at Giza was actually built over 10,000 years ago by non-Egyptians. According to Cayce, the Pyramid was not built for purposes of entombment, but as a storage place for the history of humankind from the very beginning up to the year 1998. This history is allegedly written in the languages of mathematics, geometry and astronomy.

An expert on ancient religious practices, Manly P. Hall, hypothesizes in his book *The Secret Teachings of All Ages* that the Pyramid was built by survivors of Atlantis, the lost continent. Some suggest that the leading scientists of the Atlantean civilization became aware of an impending disaster and, in order to salvage the treasures and knowledge of their age, emigrated out of the destructive reach of the cataclysm to other lands. One of these lands, theorizes Hall, was Egypt, where the Atlanteans established centres of learning, built, like their native temples, in pyramidal shapes. In these learning centres they hid their secrets, embodied in symbolic language, to be uncovered and understood only by those who were worthy of acquiring and using this sacred knowledge.

In the chapter titled 'The Initiation of the Pyramid' Hall notes that it is highly unlikely that the Egyptians erected the Pyramid because the interior walls are void of inscriptions, paintings, and other symbolism usually associated with elaborate royal decoration.

Among the tantalizing suggestions offered by Hall in this book is that the Great Pyramid might have been erected before the deluge. He bases this hypothesis on the many sea shells found at its base.

Hall also hypothesizes that during the time of the Caliph of Ma'mun, around A.D. 820, the Great Pyramid still had its outer casing stones intact. He derives this belief from the fact that the Caliph's workmen found a smooth glistening surface (the sun's rays striking the casing stones made each face of the Pyramid give off a brilliant light) with no indication of an entrance. The workmen then decided to create their own entrance by digging straight into the Pyramid. As recounted in Chapter 5, they were finally able to tunnel into one of the passageways, but found no evidence of the legendary treasures for which the Caliph had sent them to search. It is interesting to note, however, that all the casing stones, except two, have disappeared. Many archaeologists think that they are in the walls of mosques and palaces throughout Cairo, recut and repolished.

The Temple of the Mysteries

According to Hall, the Pyramid remains as the visible covenant between Eternal Wisdom and the world. Both pyramids and mounds are antetypes of the 'Holy Mountain' or the 'High Place of God'. The square base means that the Pyramid, or 'House of Wisdom', is solidly founded on Nature and its immutable laws; the angles represent Silence, Profundity, Intelligence and Truth. The south side of the Pyramid signifies Cold, the north side represents Heat, the west side symbolizes Darkness, and the east side, Light. The triangular sides typify the three-fold spiritual power.

The Great Pyramid is thought by Hall to be the 'first temple of the Mysteries'; the first structure to serve as a repository for the secret truths which are the certain foundation of all arts and sciences. Hall believes that 'the initiator', or 'the illustrious one', dressed in a blue and gold robe, carrying in his hand a seven-fold key of eternity, dwelt in the depths of the Pyramid. Men entered the portals of the Great

Pyramid, emerged as gods and became the illumined of antiquity. The drama of 'The Second Death', would be acted out in the King's Chamber, where the candidate or initiate would be symbolically crucified and buried in the sarcophagus.

This ritual would allow the initiate to experience the room as a doorway between the material world and the transcendental spheres of nature. Part of the ritual was to strike the sarcophagus producing a tone which has no counterpart in any known musical scale. After completion of the secret rites, the neophyte then was reborn, or experienced a 'second birth' and consequently experienced and gained all the knowledge of the world.

Hall feels certain that the secret room in the house of the hidden places will be rediscovered one day. This belief is shared by many mystics and psychics. Several predictions for each new year by reputable psychics claim that this room will be found and untold knowledge will once again be available to those who can understand the secrets hidden inside.

It is important to mention here that Atlantis, the so-called lost continent which Hall describes as the birthplace of the creators of the Great Pyramid, is more than a figment of some mystics' imaginations. It is actually described by Plato in his *Critias*, as formerly known as Poseidonis. He further notes that the zenith of Atlantean civilization occurred when gods walked with men.

Eleanor Merry, author of *The Flaming Door*, seems to agree with Hall that, 'the interior of the Great Pyramid was a "house of death", where the spiritual rebirth of initiation could take place and whence man could go out from the physical body in the death trance of initiation and return, in a higher consciousness to the place of his origin – that is to a vision of the spiritual world.'

Unfortunately, neither Hall nor Merry offer any concrete evidence to support their remarkable conclusions. In fact, there is no record of anyone who visited ancient Egypt having actually experienced or even watched the religious practices they described.

Dr Paul Brunton

The closest thing on record to a first-hand account is Dr Paul Brunton's description in his book, *A Search in Secret Egypt*, of his experiences during the one night he spent inside the King's Chamber of the Great Pyramid.

After going through the Egyptian bureaucratic hierarchy, Dr

Brunton succeeded in getting permission to spend a night inside the Great Pyramid.

In earlier chapters we have mentioned that the King's Chamber is strategically located inside the Pyramid. In addition to its location, the atmosphere and temperature of the chamber seems to have some mysterious significance. Says Dr Brunton, 'It has a peculiar deathlike cold which cuts to the marrow of the bone.' He adds that many say that on striking the great coffer, an unusual sound is emitted which is impossible to duplicate on any known musical instrument.

Dr Brunton recounts that on entering the King's Chamber he found a marble slab next to the large coffer which, incidentally, is exactly aligned on the north-south axis. Dr Brunton had had some training in the Egyptian religion and was also quite knowledgeable about some of the more recent discoveries in parapsychology. He had therefore prepared himself by fasting for three days before his night in the Pyramid. This, he explains, put him in a receptive frame of mind to experience whatever phenomenon existed in the Pyramid as described by Hall, Merry and others.

Sitting with his back to the great coffer, Dr Brunton decided to turn off his flashlight. The atmosphere inside the chamber, he says, was distinctly 'psychic'. There was something in the air. An unknown negative presence could be felt. Dr Brunton experienced a strong urge to leave the chamber and retreat. Instead, he forced himself to stand firm, even though grotesque and deformed entities flitted and flew about the chamber, goading Brunton's sensibility and sanity. It took every ounce of boldness and courage he possessed to fight off his ever-mounting fear. The combination of darkness and the negative presences convinced him that he would never spend another night in the Great Pyramid.

Then, as suddenly as the negative atmosphere had come, it dissipated. He felt, at first, a friendly air come alive in the chamber. Next, he discerned two figures who looked like high priests. Suddenly, inside his head, he heard the words of one of the priests. The priest was asking Brunton why he had come and if the world of mortals wasn't enough for him. Brunton answered, 'No, that cannot be.'

The priest replied, 'The way of dream will draw thee far far from the fold of reason. Some have gone upon it – and come back mad. Turn now, whilst there is yet time and follow the path appointed for mortal feet.'

Brunton insisted that he must stay. The priest who had spoken to

him turned and disappeared. The other priest requested that Brunton
lie upon the coffer, just as had the initiates of old. Brunton lay down
upon the coffer. Suddenly a force came over him. In a few seconds he
was hovering outside his body. He was in another dimension of less
stress and strain. He could see a silver luster connecting his new body
with the one lying on the coffer. He became aware of a feeling of
freedom.

Later, he found himself with the second priest who told Brunton
that he must return with a message: 'Know, my son, that in this
ancient fane lies the lost record of the early races of man and of the
Covenant which they made with the Creator through the first of His
great prophets. Know, too, that chosen men were brought here of old
to be shown this Covenant that they might return to their fellows and
keep the great secret alive. Take back with thee the warning that when
men forsake their Creator and look on their fellows with hate, as with
the princes of Atlantis in whose time this pyramid was built, they are
destroyed by the weight of their own iniquity, even as the people of
Atlantis were destroyed.'

As the priest finished speaking Brunton suddenly found himself
back in his body. He felt it to be cumbersome compared to the one he
had just inhabited. He got up, put on his jacket and checked his
watch. It was exactly twelve midnight, the hour that is customarily
associated with strange events. His subconscious had played a joke on
him. And Brunton, seeing the humour of it, laughed.

When morning arrived he made his way to the entrance. Upon
leaving, he looked up to the sun, the ancient Egyptian god Ra, and
silently gave thanks for his light.

Admittedly, Dr Brunton's account sounds like the description of a
dream incorporating details derived from readings of old religious
texts. Unfortunately, it would be extremely difficult to repeat the
doctor's experiment for one's self, since the Egyptian authorities only
grant permission to spend the night in the Pyramid in the rarest of circumstances. Whether or not one accepts Dr Brunton's story, we must
concede that it gives with the rejuvenation theories as cited in many
and varied sources.

The Papyrus of Ani

The *Papyrus of Ani*, now in the British Museum, provides the original
concept of the death and rebirth theme (the rejuvenation of the human
soul) in connection with the Great Pyramid. Better known as the

Egyptian Book of the Dead, this manuscript is thought to have been written around 1500 B.C. The translators of this papyrus, although somewhat unsure about the complete meaning and translation have, for convenience sake, agreed to interpret it as a ritual book for processing the dead, with detailed instructions for the behaviour of the disembodied spirit in the Land of the Gods. However, certain questions have been raised as to the validity of this interpretation, since the translation of the title of the papyrus can also mean, *The Book of the Great Awakening*. Viewed in a different light, the translation of the papyrus can be interpreted as the initiation rites to be performed by a neophyte who is seeking admission to a secret organization and who, upon acceptance, will gain all the worldly knowledge not afforded the commoner. Perhaps if the Great Pyramid were viewed as a temple instead of a tomb, and the *Papyrus of Ani* were then translated with this in mind, a totally different translation would develop. We believe that this text may be the key necessary to unlock the presently unfathomable secrets of the Great Pyramid.

Many renowned religious figures and ancient philosophers, including Moses, Jesus Christ and St Paul, personally acknowledged, or are acknowledged, to have their wisdom derived through the Egyptian initiation. Some of the ceremonies involving the lesser mysteries are seemingly still practised in a highly altered form by the Masons, Rosicrucians and the Christian churches, to name a few. Individuals who hinted, or even admitted, that they were Egyptian initiates include such wise men as Plato, Phythagoras, Sophocles and Cicero.

The Bible, King James version, in three separate accounts: St Matthew, chapters 26 through 28, St Mark, chapters 14 through 16, and St John, chapters 18 through 21, relates the apprehension of Christ, the crucifixion and the resurrection. Basically the story goes like this: The high priests apparently disliked Christ because his power of magic was superior to theirs, and decided to turn him over to Pilate who was the ruler of the area. After a mock trial and humiliation, Christ was crucified on a cross, along with two thieves. It is uncertain whether or not Christ actually died, but he was nonetheless removed from the cross within twenty-four hours after crucifixion and interred in a sepulchre. All this apparently occurred either on Friday or Saturday. By Sunday or Monday the sepulchre was empty and the body of Christ was gone. The uncertainty of which day Christ was placed in the vault is due to the statement that it happened the day before the sabbath. If we are to understand that the sabbath was a Saturday then it was on a Friday, if we view the sabbath to be a Sunday then it occurred on Saturday. Then the mention of the first day of the week could refer to a Sunday or a Monday. Currently we are led to believe that the interment took place on a Friday and by the following Monday Christ was gone from the tomb.

At least one stranger, perhaps two, were found by or in the sepulchre when relatives returned on the Monday to administer to the body. The strangers told the mourners that Christ had risen to go with God. Thereafter, on three separate occasions, Christ appeared to groups of people, apparently to give them a final teaching before he left, never to return. This story parallels very closely the initiation of the neophyte and the capabilities the master possesses once he becomes the keeper of the secret. The strangers at the sepulchre could very well have been high priests of the Pyramid temple lending assistance to the master who would require aid in order to return from his three-day astral projection (out-of-body) voyage, or possible state of suspended animation or extremely deep meditation.

Max Freedom Long

An entirely different theory of the building of the Great Pyramid is related by Max Freedom Long in *The Secret Science Behind Miracles*. Long tells of an English journalist, William Reginald Stewart who allegedly found a Berber tribe in the Atlas Mountains of North Africa which spoke a language containing many words similar or identical to the Hawaiian and Polynesian dialects. According to Stewart, tribal history has it that the Berber tribe was descended from twelve tribes of people living in the Sahara Desert when it was still a fertile area, with many flowing rivers. When the rivers dried up, the twelve tribes moved up into the valley of the Nile, became the rulers of Egypt and effected the construction of the Great Pyramid by helping to quarry, transport and erect the massive blocks of stone with their magic. These tribespeople then foresaw a period of intellectual darkness throughout the world and were afraid that their magic was in danger of being lost. In order to preserve the precious magic and its secret, the tribes decided to disperse to different lands. Eleven of the tribes moved into the Pacific area, while the twelfth tribe, for an unknown reason, decided to travel north and relocate in the Atlas Mountains. Apparently, the last magician of the Berber tribe to whom the secret and the magic was entrusted died before being able to

complete the training of the next individual responsible for carrying on
the tradition. To all intents and purposes the secret is now lost forever.
Supposedly the last link to it was broken around the turn of the last
century.

Davidson and Aldersmith
The Great Pyramid is considered by some to be the almanac of the
ages and the chronicler of past, present and future history. In *The
Great Pyramid: Its Divine Message*, D. Davidson and H. Aldersmith
show the extent to which the Great Pyramid was built to conform in
detail to the Pyramid allegory of Scripture.

Davidson and Aldersmith develop biblical dates from the measurements within the hollows of the Great Pyramid and claim that they
have ascertained the dates of numerous biblical events, such as the
birth of Christ (Saturday 6 October, 4 B.C.) and the crucifixion (Friday
7 April, A.D. 30).

The authors also explain that the Pyramid contains the ancient
Egyptian messianic prophecies, extending, possibly, until the end of
the world. Davidson and Aldersmith also make interesting reference
to the Great Seal of the United States, which was adopted by act of
the Continental Congress on 20 June 1782 and readopted by the new
Congress on 15 September 1789. They claim that the reverse side of
the seal depicts Cheop's Pyramid as the 'symbol of the Stone
Kingdom – with the Apex Stone – symbolic of Christ, "the headstone
of the corner" – suspended under the eye of Providence axially over
the centre of the structure thus represented as incomplete without it.'

The Great Seal of the U.S.A.
In *The Secret Teachings of All Ages*, Manly P. Hall also refers to the
Great Seal of the United States and points out that mysticism
controlled the establishment of the government. Hall shows that not
only was the Pyramid involved with the Seal, but also the symbolic
and mysterious number thirteen was incorporated in both sides of the
Seal many times over. The frequently-appearing mystical number is
apparently not only related to the original colonies forming the United
States, according to Hall, who points out that it appears on the
obverse side several times: thirteen stars above the head of the eagle;
thirteen letters in the motto 'E PLURIBUS UNUM'; thirteen leaves
and thirteen berries on the branch grasped in the eagle's right talon;
thirteen arrows clutched in his left talon; and thirteen stripes on the

Figure 10. The Great Seal.

emblem on his breast. The reverse side depicting the Great Pyramid has the motto 'ANNUIT COEPTIS', containing thirteen letters, and the pyramid itself is shown composed of thirteen layers of stone. You can substantiate these observations yourself simply by looking at the replica of the Great Seal of the United States as it appears on the one dollar paper currency of the United States. In fact, more occurrences of the symbolic number thirteen may be noted by the careful observer.

The power of the pyramid has not only survived through the milennia, but actually seems to be regaining strength. The Pristine Egyptian Orthodox Church was formed in Chicago, Illinois, in November 1963, and on 1 November 1964 held its first public service. According to an article in the March 1974 issue of *Fate Magazine*, the world's oldest monotheistic religion has been revived, probably for the first time since the last Egyptian temple ceased to exist about A.D. 600.

It should by now be apparent that there are numerous theories concerning every aspect of the Great Pyramid – from the way it was constructed, to the reason for its construction, to the identity of the people who had it constructed. One aspect of pyramidal theory which we have not touched upon is that of the geometric relationship contained in the Great Pyramid. In an article written exclusively for this book, Mr Henry Monteith deals with this fascinating facet of pyramidology.

GEOMETRY
AND
THE GREAT PYRAMID

by
Henry C. Monteith M.S.
Sandia Laboratories
Albuquerque, New Mexico

Many are the mysteries of the past, too numerous to be named, but none are more profound, and awe inspiring, than the Great Pyramid of Egypt. Two million, five hundred thousand stones, with crushing weights of two to seventy tons, rise to a height of more than four-hundred and eighty feet. This awesome structure, by its sheer bulk alone, staggers the imagination of modern construction engineers. The precision with which the stone was cut and positioned indicates that the builders of the Great Pyramid were masters of measurement. It has been estimated that it would take six years and more than one billion dollars to construct the Great Pyramid with modern technology.

Many noble efforts have been made, by investigators of the past, in an attempt to understand why the Great Pyramid was built; however, none of these efforts have yielded a conclusive answer. Personally, I believe that the Great Pyramid was built in order to record in solid stone ancient knowledge and awareness which has long since been lost. In this article, I will not be able to uncover all the mysteries which are recorded in the Great Pyramid but the inspiration which I have obtained from this magnificent structure may enable me to make some contribution to those who are seeking a deeper understanding of themselves and of our universe.

The Nature of Geometry
It is reasonable to speculate that there are two basic types of Geometry in the universe which may be classified as follows:

1. Static Geometry
2. Dynamic Geometry

We can further understand static geometry as that geometry which does not need the numbers PI (3.14) and PHI (1.618) to determine its dimensions and volume elements. Dynamic geometry can be considered as that geometry which always needs PI or PHI to determine its dimensions and volume elements.

It was believed by the ancient philosophers that the entire universe was filled with lattice network which they referred to as 'The Cosmic Web'. Each unit cell of this cosmic lattice was considered to be a cube. Indeed, the CUBE is the most perfect and balanced form that can be obtained from static geometry. The SPHERE is the most perfect and balanced form that can be obtained from dynamic geometry. I believe that all static geometrical figures can be thought of as modifications and variations of the cube, whereas, all dynamic geometrical figures can be thought of as modifications and variations of the sphere. The five regular polyhedra are shown in Figures 11-15 and one should note that they all belong to static geometry.

Figure 11.   *Figure 12.*

Figure 13.   *Figure 14.*   *Figure 15.*

Each dynamic form which appears in the physical world has its corresponding static form that appears in cosmic space. To each electron, there is associated a little cube, to each star, such as the sun, there is associated a very large cube. If the pyramid has anything to do with the structure of entities in space-time, then it must have some relationship with the cube. If it has a relationship to the cube, then static geometry must be implicit in its structure. For the same reasons, the pyramid must also have some relationship to dynamic geometry.

Assume that we have a cube, each side of which is two units long. This cube can be divided into six pyramids, each having a height of one unit, as shown in Figure 16. If we use units such that the length of one side of the Great Pyramid is two units long, then its height turns out to be the square root of PHI units long instead of one unit long. This indicates that the height of the Great Pyramid was chosen to represent dynamic geometry, on the other hand, the shape of the pyramid directly implies static geometry. The floor of the King's Chamber has the shape of a perfect Golden

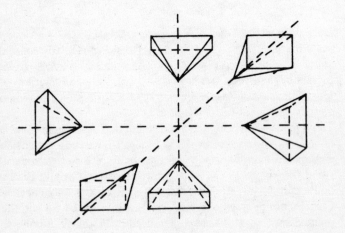

Figure 16.

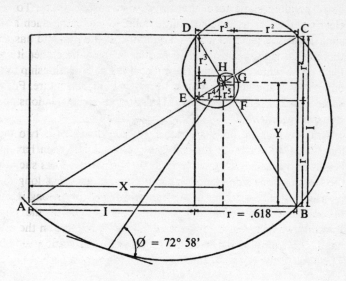

Figure 17.

Rectangle which gives all the information necessary to construct the Fibonacci series and the logarithmic spiral. The logarithmic spiral is a function of PHI and is consequently a building block of dynamic geometry. In Figure 17, we show a diagram of the logarithmic spiral, see the book by Adler for a full derivation of the spiral's mathematical aspects.[1]

Evidence of the Fibonacci series and the logarithmic spiral occur throughout the natural world. In Figure 18, we show the shell of the chambered nautilus which has the shape of a perfect logarithmic spiral. In Figure 19, we show how the perfect form of the human body can be ascertained through use of the Fibonacci series. Certain occult symbols, such as the star of David, or the five pointed star, have distances measured in Fibonacci numbers. This star is shown in Figure 20, and is sometimes called the Golden Triangle.

Throughout all the universe, the processes of life and death are common. I consider birth as a transition from static to dynamic geometry and death as a transition from dynamic to static

Figure 18. Shell of Chambered Nautilus.

geometry. A perfect dynamic sphere, like our sun, dies by radiating back into a static cube. The sun was created by having energy focused from the planes of the static cube toward a point within the cube. This idea is contrary to the modern concept of a Black Hole because a black hole implies that mass of high density can exist which will not expand into a gaseous state again. I wish to point out that a Black Hole has never been discovered, and according to my hypothesis, it will *never* be discovered. The Black Hole concept is a consequence of a failure in the postulates of modern Geometrical Physics. Just as all of the mass of a star was brought into being (by a projection) from static geometry, all of its mass must return to the static geometry from which it came (by means of radiation). The shape of the Great Pyramid denotes concentration of matter from a gaseous state (base of pyramid) to the solid state (peak of pyramid) by means of 'concentration'. It implies that a force is necessary to bring about the concentration and this force may be analogous to the power of the 'mind' to concentrate towards a single point.

Modern Physics is trying to prove that all Physics is a result of

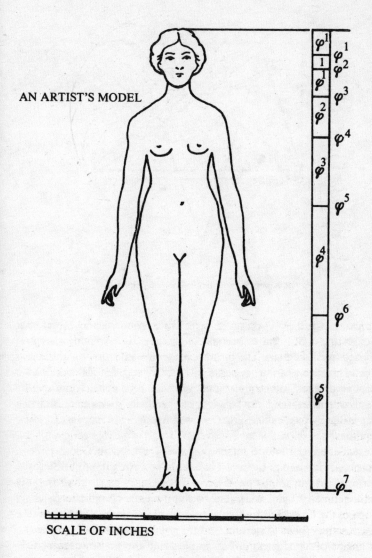

AN ARTIST'S MODEL

SCALE OF INCHES

Figure 19.

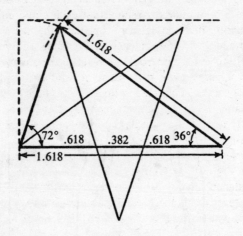

Figure 20. Golden Triangle and Five-pointed star.

pure geometry. I disagree with this concept, believing that geometry is only the 'structure' of space and that 'light' is housed within this structure. The discrete resonance phenomena, present in all of atomic physics, appears to be a consequence of light waves acting on the geometry of space. We should be able to describe the movement of light by means of dynamic geometry; and the cavities, within which light is resonating, by means of static geometry.

On the one hand, the fact that the Great Pyramid was built in such a manner as to imply 'squaring the circle' and 'cubing the sphere'[2] means to me that the ancients were trying to tell us that the static form should be shifted to the dynamic form. The pyramid can easily be shifted to a cone and the cube can be likewise shifted to a sphere. The cone is a perfect representation of the dynamic concentration of energy. This implies that the shape of the cone is connected with creation in some manner. On the other hand, the logarithmic spiral gives the impression of outward 'expansion'. Consequently, I assume that it is connected with the transition from the dynamic geometrical state to the static geometrical state.

Another interesting point may be brought out by considering the volume of the Great Pyramid, using units such that each side is two units long. A cube, with each side being two units long, has a volume of 8 cubic units. Assume that each cubic unit contains a unit of energy, then we can say that the cube has a volume of 8 units containing 8 units of energy. Six times the volume of the Great Pyramid of Egypt contains 8 times the square root of PHI units of volume; thus, it can represent 8 times the square root of PHI energy units. This means that the pyramid represents more energy than is necessary to sustain an associated cube. This implies that energy is contained within the cube; consequently, we assume that this energy is light energy.

From Newton we understand that for every action there is an equal and opposite reaction. Since the universe must always be in perfect balance, it is logical to assume that there must be a reaction or counterpart to all perceived forces and entities. For example, in Physics we know that if we have a positive charge located at some

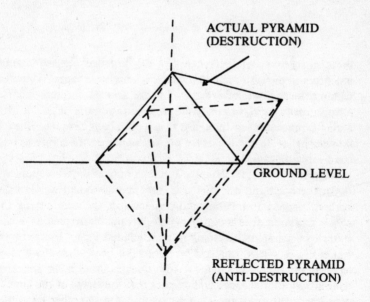

ACTUAL PYRAMID
(DESTRUCTION)

GROUND LEVEL

REFLECTED PYRAMID
(ANTI-DESTRUCTION)

Figure 21. The destruction and anti-destruction pyramids.

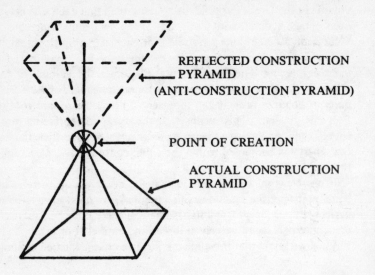

Figure 22. Construction and anti-construction Pyramids. .

distance above ground, we can plot the field between the charge and ground by assuming that there is another charge, which is negative, located an equal distance below ground. In other words, when a positive charge is present, a negative charge must also be implicity present, even though it is not physically present. Thus, I assume that there are implicitly present one or more antipyramids to the Great Pyramid.

Because of its asymmetry the Pyramid implies two directions of thought projection, one towards the apex, which we take to represent material creation, and one towards the base which we take to represent destruction. The anti-destruction pyramid is back-to-back to the actual pyramid and is located below ground (see Figure 21). The anti-construction pyramid is peak to peak with the actual pyramid and is located above the apex (see Figure 22). The joint action of the construction and anti-construction pyramids bring about creation, the joint action of the destruction and anti-destruction pyramids bring about the expansion and death of that which has been created. Destruction and construction interact

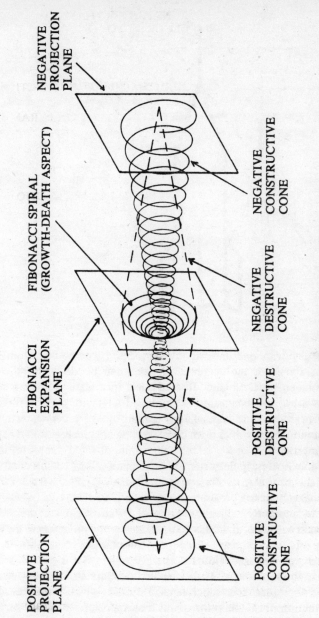

Figure 23. Dynamic Life-Death Cycle, Pyramid shifted to Cone.

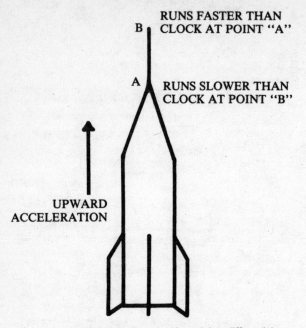

Figure 24. Rocket ship and time differential.

cyclically with one another. Consequently, we see that from the Great Pyramid, the same conclusions can be drawn that were determined by Dr Walter Russell while in a state of cosmic consciousness.[3] We illustrate the combined life-death cycle in Figure 23. These dynamic cone shapes remind one of a very interesting observation that comes from considerations in General Relativity.

Suppose that there is a rocket ship, located far from any heavenly bodies, in deep space. Let us place a long rod on the front of this rocket ship as illustrated in Figure 24), then we will cause the rocket ship to accelerate upwards with a constant acceleration. From General Relativity, it is calculated that the clock at the end of the rod runs faster than the clock located at the point where the rod joins the rocket ship. From conclusions such as this, it is determined that space-time acts very much like a curved space (dynamic geometry). It is further determined, from General Relativity, that the space-time diagram, which describes the accelerating rocket ship with respect to the rest of the universe, has the form of two cones, apex to apex as illustrated in Figure 25).

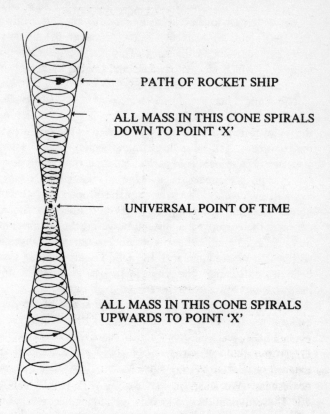

Figure 25. Cone of accelerating rocket ship (general relativity).

This is directly analogous to what has been deduced from the Great Pyramid. This space-time cone has very interesting inter-pretations: The point where the apexes of the two cones meet is the anchor for all action in the system. The ancient Hindus believed that the entire being of all created things are balanced about a single point. All events which happen in the domain of the space-time cone of the space ship happen simultaneously in the point at which the two cones meet. In other words, the past and the future have no meaning at the point at which the two cones meet. 'All that was is, now; and all that shall be is, now!' Indeed, this is an eternal and cosmic concept of which we, at present, understand but little. From the point of view of the accelerating space ship, all heavenly bodies which are located in the upper cone accelerate downward to the apex and all heavenly bodies located in the lower cone accelerate upward to the apex. This is directly analogous to the manner in which atomic particles are created by accelerating light towards the point of concentration.

The Time Theory of Nikolai Kozyrev[4] is also implied in the Great Pyramid of Egypt. Asymmetry is the cornerstone of this theory of time and asymmetry is implied in the Great Pyramid by the number PHI. The logarithmic spiral is an asymmetrical structure. If a system is in perfect balance, there is no possible way for motion to appear in it. One of the primary purposes of asymmetry in nature is to set up the proper conditions to bring about motion. According to Kozyrev, time has the ability to decrease the entropy of a system; however, the action of time upon a system is so minute that it goes undetected in the physical system with which we are familiar. If the action of time upon a system does become noticeable, the engineers just attribute it to system perturbations. In the Great Pyramid of Egypt, the action of the flow of time has been amplified, by the shape of the pyramid, to make it capable of preserving organic matter. Time-flow and Bioplasma are just different terms used to describe the same mysterious force which is responsible for the creation and maintenance of all material systems. According to Kozyrev, bioplasma has the ability to increase the energy of a system but it is unable to affect the momentum of a system.

Bioplasma should have properties which are just the reverse of nuclear energy. It was Dr Wilhelm Reich who first experimented with this idea in what he referred to as 'The Oranur Experiment'.[5] In this experiment it was found that bioplasma reacted violently with radioactive material, producing a by-product that was extremely dangerous to life for a short period of time. However, it was also found that the radioactivity was reduced by the action of the bioplasma. This experiment gives evidence that bioplasma is definitely a creative force which acts in the opposite direction to nuclear force. In the words of Kozyrev: 'If mechanics enables us some day to detect and control vital processes outside organic life, operating machines will renovate (and not only exhaust) the world's potentialities. Thus, a genuine harmony between man and nature may be established. Abstract as this dream sounds, it has a realistic basis.'

From these considerations, we understand that 'Time' is simply the geometrical aspect of bioplasma, expressing as static geometry; whereas, concentration (the focusing of energy) is its dynamic aspect, expressing rhough dynamic geometry. The reciprocal action between dynamic and static geometry bring about the processes of decay and death, together with construction and life. In Figure 23 the Life-Death cycle is illustrated. The static planes house the causes of creation, and the focus points embody the effects of creation. In other words, all causes in the universe are inherent in static geometry, whereas, all effects are grounded in dynamic geometry.

Before these ideas can be fully accepted and utilized by modern science, they must be put in detailed analytical form. This requires a deep understanding of the laws governing the creative processes of nature. Thus far, this necessary understanding has not been obtained by those, like myself, who are investigating the subject. It is my belief that the next revolution in science will be along these lines and that it is necessary that the energy responsible for creating the universe be incorporated into modern science before the unsolved problems which science faces today can be solved. For example, there can be no Unified Field Theory until the nature of the biplasma has been comprehended. A complete and detailed study of the Great Pyramid, by competent scientists with the bioplasma in mind, may help to throw more light upon our ignorance.

References

1. Adler, *Mathematics For Science and Engineering* (McGraw-Hill).

2. Tompkins, Peter, *Secrets of the Great Pyramid* (Harper and Row, New York, 1971).

3. Russell, Walter, *The Secret of Life* (University of Science and Philosophy, Waynesboro, Virginia).

4. Kozyrev, Nikolai, *Possibility of Experimental Study of the Properties of Time* (Joint Publications Research Service, NTIS, Springfield, Virginia, 1968).

5. Reich, Wilhelm, *Cosmic Superimposition* (The Wilhelm Reich Foundation, Orgonon, Rangeley, Maine, 1951).

Peter Tompkins in his book *Secrets of the Great Pyramid*, compiles a fantastic storehouse of information computed from the dimensions of Cheops pyramid, by various astute authorities during the late 1800s and early 1900s. These range from the Pyramids being a 'perfect geodetic benchmark' whose angles completely enclosed the delta region in its entirety, to the height of the Pyramid being a billionth part of the distance to the sun. The Great Pyramid has been shown by engineers, mathematicians and the like to embody the value for Pi (π) equalling 3.144..., which closely resembles the exact accepted equivalent of 3.14159 which was only correctly worked out in the sixth century A.D. The Egyptians were apparently well aware that the earth was a globe and possibly from this they determined that there were 365 days in a year and that the perimeter of the base of the Pyramid was an exact fraction of the circumference of the earth.

However, Tompkins does not even attempt to explain to what purpose these sophisticated and precise calculations were put.

The Secrets of the Sphinx

Mystical speculation has not been solely confined to the Great Pyramid, but has also revolved around the Great Sphinx, which stands its enigmatic guard less than a quarter of a mile southeast of the Pyramid, close to the valley building of Chephren. Many people still believe that the Pyramid contains several hidden chambers and passageways which connect to the Sphinx and the surrounding pyramids. The discovery of the existence of these chambers and corridors will, most mystics fervently believe, solve the thousands of mysteries which have piled up throughout the ages.

It is also thought that the adept would have to gain entrance to the secret chambers of the Great Pyramid through a door hidden between the paws of the Sphinx. This secret door could only be opened by the master who possessed the knowledge of a hidden trigger, which would supposedly spring open a bronze gate. The adept would then have to begin his first lesson as he traversed the mazelike passageways. The correct choice of each turn and section of the corridors would immediately begin the initiation procedures necessary to lead to his ultimate rebirth as a god.

Of course, no such secret entrance has ever been found. It is thought by some that if the entrance ever actually existed, it was sealed forever during one of the scores of restorations perpetrated by many successive civilizations.

Another theory is that this secret entrance may actually be *directly beneath* the Sphinx. When the necessity arose to abandon the use of the Great Pyramid as the temple of secret initiation, the Sphinx was set in its sentinel position over the entrance and is still guarding it to this very day.

Still others suggest that the Sphinx itself is the actual door to the entrance of the secret passageways, and the execution of some special, unknown code or ritual would reposition the great statue so that the entranceway would be revealed.

Perhaps the most famous association with the Great Sphinx is the riddle: 'What animal goes on four feet in the morning, on two feet at noon, and on three feet in the evening?' This riddle is actually attributable to a closely-related Winged Greek sphinx, who guarded the road to Thebes. This sphinx would ask this riddle of all who passed before it and would destroy those who could not answer correctly. Allegedly, the first man to give the correct answer was Oedipus, who thus saved himself from destruction. The answer is 'Man himself, who in childhood crawls upon his hands and feet, in manhood stands erect, and in old age shuffles along, supporting himself on a staff.'

Another answer to this riddle, involving the Pythagorean values of numbers, is afforded by the science of numerology. The three numbers, four, two and three total nine, the natural number of man. Four represents man in his ignorance, two symbolizes his development as an intelligent being, and three signifies his final step towards mastering the universal knowledge of the spiritual person.

The Pyramid as a Library

One particularly interesting theory as to the purpose of the Great Pyramid (and other major pyramids around the world) is that it was built as a massive and indestructible storehouse in which to record and preserve throughout eternity the wisdom of the peoples who built it. This information would have been recorded in the form of hieroglyphics which are highly vulnerable to errors of translation and interpretation.

The major appeal of this theory is its practicality. It is obvious that books are a risky form of recording information, since they are so highly perishable. And once a book is destroyed, if no copy exists, the knowledge and information contained in that book is lost forever, unless the author is able to accurately replicate it.

Thus it seems likely that the ancients, with their highly developed scientific and artistic culture, would wish to preserve their knowledge in an indestructible fashion. It has been suggested that the reason that later civilizations were unable to interpret the hieroglyphs is that the ancients made the mistake of believing that symbolism which was obvious to them would be equally obvious to other people from other places in other times.

That the builders of such a great civilization could be so short-sighted seems more reasonable when one recalls the plate installed in the NASA space vehicle intended to convey a symbolic message to any possible inhabitants of other planets where the space ship might land. This message incorporated the language of astronomy, atomic chemistry, and simple pictures of earthlings to convey information about our universe to those who might exist on other worlds. More than likely, if any such extraterrestrial being did discover the vehicle and try to decipher the plaque, they might find it totally inscrutable. The information contained in the various parts of the Great Pyramid is exactly this type of symbolism – obvious to the creator, but incomprehensible to the reader from another age or another world.

Certainly we have proof that it is a human instinct to want to preserve knowledge for posterity. For instance, even prior to the Christian era, about three-quarters of a million of the most valuable books of the ancient world were assembled from the four corners of the known universe and housed in specially constructed buildings in Alexandria for the sole purpose of preserving the knowledge of all the then extant civilizations. These books were of wood, stone, parchment, terra cotta, vellum and even wax.

This library was destroyed in a series of deliberately-set fires, the second of which was ordered by the Caesar reigning in A.D. 389 for the purpose of destroying the Alexandrian fleet in its own harbour. The volumes surviving the pyromaniacal action were later immolated by the Christians in obedience to Theodosius' edict ordering the destruction of the *Serapeum*, the building sacred to Serapis. This building is thought to have contained the library that Marcus Antonius presented to Cleopatra to compensate for the parts destroyed in the first fire, which occurred in A.D. 51.

Books which might have survived the series of fires could have been brought to other parts of Egypt, or India, but all known records of their whereabouts are lost and with them, presumably, the greatest collection of ancient wisdom the world has ever known. If, as is highly probable, information revealing the secrets of the Pyramid was contained in the books deposited in the Alexandria library, it is lost to us forever, and the mystery of the Pyramids will remain so throughout eternity.

We have, in this chapter, presented a variety of accounts of the origins and purpose of the Great Pyramid. We believe that it is immaterial whether or not these stories are true. The point is, there is much about the Pyramid which is little known or understood. These narratives achieve a heightened curiosity about the purpose and functions of the Pyramid. They give us a new sense of wonder and mystery about the remarkable structure and its effect on humankind.

8

The Struggle for the Pyramid Patent

by
Karl Drbal

Karl Drbal is a retired radio engineer who had pioneered radio and television in Czechoslovakia. Now in his seventies, nearly half of his life has been devoted to the theory of regeneration of energy. His interest and research in the field of unusual energy forms is, like his razor blades, keen and sharp. This chapter was prepared by Mr Drbal in Prague, Czechoslovakia on 12 February 1974, especially for this book.

This is the story of patent No. 91304, a strange invention which has gone around the whole world — an invention which more or less indicates that the cavity of a little cardboard model of the Great Pyramid of Cheops can affect the steel edge of a razor blade.

It should be stressed that the patent application, which was filed in Prague, Czechoslovakia, in 1949, was granted only in 1959. Since the normal time taken by the Patent Examination Commission is between one and three years, it is obvious that the Commission considered the invention before them a rather extraordinary one.

During the ten-year application period I was forced to develop new scientific arguments to explain how this extremely simple device, without any evident source of energy, can affect the steel edge of a razor blade which has been dulled by repeated use in shaving.

Originally, when I applied for the patent, it was almost a joke for me and my friends who, like myself, are radio engineers, and who encouraged me to apply just to find out how the patent office would react to issuing a patent on a 'Pharaoh's shaving device'. However, I must emphasize that these friends were totally persuaded, as I was, after having used a single razor blade stored in the pyramid-regenerator for more than one-hundred daily shaves, that this strange device really works.

It was another matter to persuade the patent examiners not only that it works but – and much more difficult – *how* it works.

Throughout the ten years during which the commission considered the application, I devoted myself to studying all the possible microwave, cosmic and telluric relations between the resonant cavity of a Cheops-pyramid model, constructed in dielectric material (cardboard or other), and the working of the crystalitic structure of the edge of the razor blade. I also studied the connection of the very low earth magnetic field, because one condition of the patent is that the blade must lie by its longitudinal axis in the direction of the horizontal component of the earth's magnetic field.

My employment in a large radio research institute was of the greatest importance to me during this time, since I had easy access to all the necessary technical literature of the whole world. Step-by-step, during my ten year fight with the patent examiners, I was able to realize a theory (or hypothesis) about the energization of the resonant cavity of the little pyramid-model by cosmic microwaves (principally from the sun) with help from the concentrating earth magnetic field. Having ascertained the technical possibility of such energy-feeding of the pyramid, I was then able to persuade the examiners that, indeed, the Pharaoh Chufev (Cheops) has nothing in common with the razor blades and that the whole thing is not nonsense.

During this period, I constructed a cardboard model, 'type Cheops', 8cm high, base line 12.5cm (one inch is equal to approximately 2.54cm), which I presented to the chief patent examiner (an excellent metallurgical specialist). Since the model worked entirely to his satisfaction throughout the ten-year period, he was able to prove, by his own experience, that the invention is not a mystification. He was therefore obliged to defend my invention to the examining commission. I am sure that without the help of this honest examiner the 'strange' patent No. 91304 would not exist today.

The patent was conceived for the 'Cheops-type', where the baseline can be easily calculated by multiplying the height of the pyramid by $\frac{Pi}{2}$ (i.e., 1.57079), which is exactly specified in the patent description. However, the invention is not limited to this specific form since I have found, through an extremely large number of different experiences, that other pyramidal shapes (types) are also able to affect the razor-blade edge in the same manner as the Cheops-type. I have specified this possibility in the patent description, which also indicates why (with regard to my hypothesis) the pyramid-model cavity works (or is supposed to work) on the fine crystalitic structure of the edge.

The title of the patent specification is as follows: 'Device for maintaining the sharpness of razor blades and razors.' (It is made very clear here that the device is *not* a *sharpener*, which is only a 'symbolic' definition, but a *regenerator*.)

The last paragraph of the description, containing my explanations provided for a better understanding of my hypothesis, which was accepted by the examiners, follows herewith:

This invention was specially tested for a specific pyramid-shape device, but is not restricted only to this one specific form, meaning that it can also be valuable for other geometric forms of dielectric material, used in the manner described in this invention, explained in the following working definition:

In the space enclosed by this form, an automatic regeneration process will start, affecting the razor blade edge, produced only by the said cavity (this means that the excitation of this cavity is only produced by the surrounding cosmic and terrestrial field, e.g., electric, magnetic, electromagnetic, gravitic, corpuscular and perhaps other fields and energies, not yet defined). This process, acting on the razor-blade edge by producing a diminution of the number of inner disturbances (dislocations, provoked by the shaving process) in the lattice bonds of the microcrystalitic structure of the edge-shape (it must be steel of the best quality), have as a result caused a *regeneration* of the edge-material of its fine, crystalitic structure; a regeneration which operates a renovation of the mechanical and physical properties of the razor-blade edge, removing the 'fatigue' of the material, issued from the shaving action, and all this only if the crystal lattice disturbances are of elastic type and not of definitive type (e.g., mechanical destruction-action on the edge).

Let me comment here that a necessary supposition is that the blade steel is of very first quality, so that the deformation of the micro-structure-blade-edge, produced by multiple shavings, is not of definitive, but of elastic, character.

The pyramid (type Cheops, or other form), or any appropriate resonator for the same use, has only to produce an acceleration in the restoration of the elastic deformation to the original (or nearly original) state of the edge; acceleration which, instead of the normal (without the regeneration device) fifteen to thirty days, is improved in only twenty-four hours! This is the real secret of the pyramid-resonant cavity action on the edge of the razor blade.

One more very interesting effect was discovered by Professor Dr Carl Benedicks, of Stockholm (see: *Metallkundliche Berichte*, Verlage Technik, Berlin, 1952, Tome II. 'Aenderung der Festigkeit von Metallen und Nichtmetallen durch eine benetzende Flüssigkeit' – the so-called Flüssigkeitseffekt), the 'liquid-stain effect' which produces on steel a non-corrosive but steel-firmness reducing action (water acting on steel can reduce its firmness by as much as 22 per cent!). This fact is very inhibitive in the edge micro-cavities, from where it is difficult (one might even say impossible) to expel the harmful water dipole molecules.

The pyramid (or other appropriate resonant cavity) is the only device which can do the helpful job on the razor-blade-edge-crystal gaps of driving out the dipole water molecules by resonant action on this dipole; we can, therefore, symbolically say that it dehydrates the edge of the razor blade.

That such an action on the dipole-molecules of water is possible in a resonant cavity, fed with appropriate micro-wave energy, was proved by the scientists Born and Lertes (see: *Archiv. der elektrischen Uebertragung*, 1950, Heft 1, s.33-35. 'Der Born-Lertessche Drehfeldeffekt in Dipolflüssigkeiten im Gebiet der Zentimeterwellen'). It was found that the microwaves of centimetre-wavelength and their harmonics can produce an accelerated rotation of the water dipole-molecules, and this effect can have as a result the dehydration process – the 'driving out' of water dipole-molecules from the smallest cavities and projecting them in the open air. This is exactly the process of electromagnetic dehydration.

The question, then, is raised as to why the pyramid models must be made from dielectrical materials. The answer is simply that micro-waves can penetrate this material and energize (feed) the resonant cavity. This is a very old discovery (see: *Journal of Applied Physics*, Vol. 10, June 1939, pp. 391-398; Richtmyer, R.D., Stanford University, California 'Dielectric Resonators').

It should be pointed out that in microwave techniques the microwave resonator should be fed by some small antenna or by a coupling hole. The pyramid can be built without such a hole, and unobstructed in function, I have explicated that the microwaves can penetrate through dielectric material (if microwaves really are in action here). This was confirmed experimentally by microwave technicians as, for example, *Electronique, Revue Technique Electronique*, No. 118, Sept. 1956, pp. 10-13, Henry Copin, Ingénieur au service des transmissions militaires: 'De l'existence possible d'ondes stationnaires dans les cellules vivantes.' (The possibility of standing-wave excitation in the living cells.) This author supposes each living cell to be a microwave resonator and, as a radio technician, explains the mechanism of cavity-excitation with its surrounding walls consisting of dielectric or semiconductor material.

The objection of the examiners that the pyramid-shape in microwave devices is not usual was easy to reject with the aid of some literature I presented (for example: *Zeitschrift für angewandte Physik*, Band 6, Heft 11, 1954, s.499-507, Gerhard Piefke 'Die Ausbreitung elektromagnetischer Wellen in einem *Pyramidentrichter*').

I was also invited by the Office to tell them something about the amount of the microwave energy coming from the Sun, eventually reflected by the earth, with regard to the possibility of resonant action on the micro-structure-grid of the razor blade edge. I proved, by scientific evidence, that with the help of the pyramidal resonant cavity, or by the bunching effect of a pyramid horn, this energy can be sufficient. I further proved that the energy needed for steel-crystal grid action on dislocations is only in the amount of 1 to 1.5 ev (electronvolts – one electronvolt representing the energy of 1.6×10^{-19} watt seconds), which means that this energy is very low and can be easily overcome by spheric and technic action (microwaves, produced by technical devices in the hollow of the pyramid). See, for example, P. Fischer and Kochendörfer 'Plastiche Eigenschaften von Kristallen (Kristallgittern) und metallischen Werkstoffen' (Plastic characters of steel crystal grids).

My hypothesis, elaborated for the Patent Office (I do not affirm here that it is the only one possible) explains also why the regenerating pyramid should not be placed too near to room walls, greater metal masses, or to numerous electric devices (definitely not on television sets).

In order to explain, on a simple level, how the pyramid works on the razor blade edge, I like to compare it to the photo exposure meter which, like the pyramid, acts without any artificial source of energy – only with the impetus of visible sun light. The only difference between the two devices is that mine acts with an invisible Sun light.

The above comprises the main portion of my hypothesis for the Patent Office, the result of which was that at the end of 'only' ten years of examination, and proof of real functioning provided by the chief examiner himself, the patent was issued.

By now it should be apparent that there is no magic involved in the functioning of the razor-blade pyramid, nor of the mummification model pyramid. Rather, there are two main factors at work here:

1. Fast dehydration (which, as I explained earlier, also works in some manner on the razor blade).
2. Action on micro-crystal lattice of inorganic matter (fine layer of steel), or action on the structure or microstructure of organic matter, living or dead, sterilization which means killing of micro-organisms. It must be emphasized that this action can, in extreme cases, actually kill small animals by rapid dehydration and some 'devitalization'.

I have spoken briefly about models other than Cheops, the elevation of which is about 51° 51′ 51″. (Piazzi Smyth, England; Abbé Moreux, France; L. Seidler, U.S.S.R.). I, and also some French experimenters, have found that a very good functioning pyramid model can also be constructed with a 65° elevation (what in Europe is approximately the magnetic inclination angle). I named this type the Inclination-Pyramid.

Upright to the wall of this model we found an elevation angle of 25°; this form represents a very good mummification pyramid, with great wall surface, which I called the Contra-Inclination Pyramid. With all these models I made a great number of mummifications, but for the razor-blade I prefer the Cheops model.

In the No. 9, 1973 edition of the journal *Esotera* (BRD), on pp. 799-800, Hans Joachim Höhn confirms the functioning of the Cheops pyramid on razor blades, but proposes his own model with an elevation angle of 69° 20′, base line 15 cm., height 22.2 cm., with which, he says, he obtained 196 very good shaves, using a Wilkinson-Sword blade.

Another experimenter, in an article entitled 'In der Pyramide wird jede Klinge wieder scharf' (Every razor blade recovers its sharpness in the pyramid model), essays his own improvement.

Antoine Bovis

The indirect initiator of my experiments with the cardboard pyramid models was Mr Antoine Bovis, a Frenchman for whom intuition, rather than scientific evidence, was fully sufficient: he experimented with both the divining rod and the pendulum and, probably through the use of the pendulum, found the possibility of mummification in small Cheops models.

Travelling in Egypt, Mr Bovis visited the Great Pyramid and found, in the Royal Chamber, which is one-third of the entire height of the pyramid, mummified animals. In an intuitional flash, Mr Bovis deduced that the pyramid had powers of mummification and, upon his return home, reproduced scale models of the Great Pyramid, using scales of 1:1000 (15cm high) and 1:500 (30cm high), the baseline calculated by multiplying the height by $\frac{\pi}{2}$ or approximately 1.57.

Bovis was sure that his seemingly mad experiments with mummification would succeed without the help of any technical literature, physical reviews or other scientific data. For him the small pendulum of his own patented construction was sufficient. For Bovis it wes easy to have the pendulum patented, since in France, unlike in Czechoslovakia, it is possible to obtain a patent without providing any technical explanation. As long as the invention is something new, it is not necessary to prove that it works!

I first came across the name Antoine Bovis in a little radiaesthesic booklet in which appeared his different lectures, given in radiaesthesic circles of Nizza, about his (according to him) numerous, and especially his little 'Special magnetic pendulum of Bovis', which, he says, is the best of all. Following each paragraph, there was another 'Law of radiaesthesia action', the only one possible, discovered by Bovis himself.

In one of his lectures, he spoke about his mummification experiments with Cheops pyramid cardboard models, because he had found in these models, with his pendulum, 'the same radiations', as in the King's Chamber of the Great Pyramid. Evidently, his models worked! Dead organic matter, meat, eggs, and small dead animals were as perfectly mummified as were the animals he found in the Pyramid at Gizeh.

Because it was relatively simple to ascertain if Bovis' claims were fiction or reality, I constructed a Cheops model, 30cm high, in cardboard 3mm thick (scale 1:500) and, to my great astonishment, I, like Mr Bovis, was able to create mummifications – to repeat with success his mummification experiments – mummifying beef, calf or lamb meat, eggs, flowers and even small dead reptiles such as frogs, snakes, lizards, etc.

I began a correspondence with Mr Bovis, informing him of my experiments. We exchanged some agreeable correspondence, although I felt that he was a little 'too magic' for me, a radiotechnician. He claimed to find with his pendulum radiations in everything he touched.

By his letter I came to know that Bovis had an ironmongery shop at Nizza (Quincaillerie, Bovis and Passeron) and that he considered himself a great inventor in radiaesthesic laws and also of devices of all kinds. He was also the founder of another firm, Artisanat A. Bovis, Nice, which manufactured radiaesthesia devices. Some of his products included the pendulum 'paradiamagnetic', a radioscope, biometer, plates, 'magnetics' for mummification and action on liquids, magnetic and nonmagnetic material, all having been constructed and on the market since 1931.

I eventually began to make a great many mummifications with pyramids of different forms and shapes, but mostly with the Cheops type. In collaboration with Mr Martial, from Valenciennes, I published my findings in French and Belgian radiaesthesic journals, e.g., *La Revue Internationale de Radisthesie*, No. 7, Avril 1948, pp. 54-57 (France); *La Radiesthesie Pour Tous*, No. 12, 1949, pp. 377-379 (Belgium), and through these articles contacted other French radiaesthesists interested in mummification by Cheops pyramid models.

I was at last, as a radiotechnician, forced to admit that there is something very strange in the mummification phenomenon – some energy must evidently be concentrated in the pyramid model. In 'looking out for the nature of this energy' I was encouraged to make further 'mad experiments' – to place a new razor blade of good quality (the Blue Gillette) in the cardboard Cheops pyramid. If there was a blunting of the edge, this would provide me with physical evidence of some concentrated force acting in the pyramid.

And so began my razor-blade adventure with the Cheops model. My assumption that the blade in the pyramid would lose its sharpness was false. Just the contrary occurred, and when I had shaved myself comfortably fifty times, I was forced to admit that there was something very wrong in my supposition.

My first razor-blade experiment was made with a Cheops type pyramid 15cm high (scale 1:1000), the blade was poised horizontally north-south on its longitudinal axis and one-third above the base; two sides of the pyramid were oriented in the same manner.

Through numerous experiments I found that for this purpose a cardboard pyramid 8cm high, or a styreen pyramid 7cm high is sufficient. Years later this styreen model was fabricated by a plastic material factory, but only some hundreds of pieces were produced before they refused to continue the manufacture. Although I do not know all the circumstances causing the refusal, I can speculate that perhaps a great factory of razor blades, distressed at the possibility of having a consumer use a single blade one hundred times or more, persuaded the plastic factory to discontinue manufacture of the item.

Of course, it is very easy for anyone who wishes to do so to make this little pyramid. It is difficult for me to guess how many home-made pyramids exist in the U.S.S.R., but I can testify that of the thousands and thousands of users who have written me concerning the pyramid, not one has complained, but a great number have written with great enthusiasm.

The last twenty-five years have been for me a long experimental sequence, with each shaving itself an experimental experience which has sometimes informed me, by unexpected changes in the sharpness of the blade, of some meteorological or cosmic disturbances. The blade edge in the pyramid is a 'living entity', in contact with the environmental field – often after a day when I received a poor shave I was surprised the next day by receiving, from the same blade, an excellent shave.

To judge the sharpness of the blade I have introduced a scale with six degrees: No. 6 = excellent, No. 5 = very good, No. 4 = good, No. 3 = sufficient, No. 2 = fair and No. 1 = insufficient. In the first five years and three months of my experiment (from 3 March 1949 to 6 July 1954) the average value of one blade was 105 daily shaves (using only eighteen blades of different brands) and I achieved as many as 200, 170, 165, 111 and 100 shaves with a single blade. In twenty-five years I used a total of sixty-eight blades.

I have corresponded about this strange patent with experimenters in a number of countries in Europe, and also in the U.S.A., South America, Australia, New Zealand and Iceland. Great interest has also been expressed by researchers in the U.S.S.R. For example, in the *Komsomolskaja Pravda* of 10 October, 1970, (and reprinted in the Moscow journal *Heureka* in 1973) Mr Malinov, CSC, wrote an interesting article about, to use his expression, 'a strange invention'.

As a physicist, Mr Malinov has formed a logical explanation of the functioning of the pyramid, by using electromagnetic theory combined with the earth's magnetic field and also with the 'Lorentz forces'. I have also learned that my little pyramid is, in home-made form, of customary use in the U.S.S.R.

My experimentation has led me to write some articles about the regenerating pyramid for popular science journals and other periodicals in Eastern Europe. I have also spoken on a radio broadcast and even appeared in a television interview. All of this publicity has brought me a very great number of friendly letters.

In conclusion, I wish everyone who uses or will use this invention two hundred or more shaves with the same blade.

9

Transform Yourself With Pyramid Energy

In 1968, a research project was undertaken to attempt to discover once and for all whether or not there are any secret chambers in the pyramids of Egypt.

Dr Luis Alvarez, who developed and directed the project, had specifically designed an instrument which would record cosmic rays passing through the pyramid's masonry. He had gained the idea for this instrument from reading *The Great Pyramid in Fact and Theory*, in which its author, William Kingsland, suggests transmitting radio waves 5 metres long, and recording the strength of the transmitted wave from the King's Chamber to the outer surface of Cheops' pyramid. This method, postulates Kingsland, would reveal whether any hidden chamber existed.

Alvarez then further hypothesized that cosmic rays bombarding our planet twenty-four hours a day from outer space, lose energy in proportion to the density and thickness of the objects through which they pass, and built his instrument accordingly.

Instead of following Kingsland's suggestion and attempting to discover a secret chamber in Cheops' pyramid, Alvarez chose instead the pyramid of Chephren, because he thought it more likely that this structure would contain a hidden passage, and because it was thought to have been built later than Cheops' pyramid and consequently might have a more sophisticated interior architectural design.

Having designed this device, Alvarez then put together a team of scientists from a total of twelve agencies from the United Arab Republic and the United States (one of which was the U.S. Atomic Energy Commission). With the combined weight of these respectable agencies backing them, the researchers naturally had the necessary financial and technical support vital to the execution of this ambitious project – a project which, they hoped, would ultimately realize the Egyptologists' dream: the finding of the sarcophagus of the Pharaoh.

In September of 1968, the team recorded millions of cosmic ray trajectories on special magnetic tape designed to be evaluated by computers. The tapes were first analyzed by a computer in Cairo. The results clearly indicated the location of the faces, edges and corners of the Pyramid, but no hidden chamber was located in the 35-degree conical scan of the rays which were recorded in the central chamber.

Additional, more precise computer analyses of the tape and its millions of pieces of information followed. According to Dr Amr Gohed, the head of the Cairo group, each time the tape was reanalyzed by an IBM 1130 computer at the Ein Shams University in Cairo, a different pattern would emerge, with prominent features which should have appeared every time now missing.

A duplicate copy of the computer tapes was taken to the United States by Dr Alvarez' assistant, Dr Laurin Yazolino. These were analyzed by a highly sophisticated computer at Berkeley, California, which, according to Alvarez, consistently reported the same results through analysis after analysis.

Dr Gohed agrees that the differing results obtained from the Cairo computer analyses appear to be scientifically impossible and states that there is either a substantial error in the geometry of the Pyramid which affects the recordings, or that some mysterious force, which defies the laws of science, is at work in the Pyramid.

The idea that there is some inexplicable or unknown energy which is peculiar to the pyramid shape is not a new one. In fact, the basic contention of the *Papyrus of Ani* (see Chapter 7) is that the god who is sleeping in the soul of each person is awakened by the power, or energy, of the pyramid.

Stimulation of Psychic Power

Although twentieth century mystics do not necessarily believe that the pyramid shape can actually arouse dormant gods, many feel that psychic powers are stimulated or heightened by the use of a home-made pyramid as a meditation area. Apparently, psychics who use pyramids in this fashion have achieved an altered state of consciousness more rapidly than they would have otherwise. They claim that the powers of the pyramid work best when they situate themselves in either a prone or sitting position along the north-south axis beneath the apex of the pyramid.

The experiences of psychics who have used the pyramid seem to vary considerably. Some report that they receive answers or visions, or both, in response to a particular set of questions or problems while they are still inside the pyramid. Others claim that they feel only serenity and integration with cosmic forces during their pyramid sessions; that it is only after they have emerged from the pyramid that spiritual impressions and psychic perceptions virtually flood forth from their consciousnesses. Many psychics believe that strong energy forces exist within the pyramid which, during meditation sessions, clear psychic passages which may have become blocked.

E.S.P. Laboratory, a psychical-research organization based in Los Angeles, California, is conducting experiments in which the pyramid shape is actually used as an incubator for thought-forms. The organization's director, Al Manning, explains that the pyramid form functions as a geometric amplifier which increases the power of prayer or strengthens the spiritual request of a religious devotee. Members of this worldwide organization are ostensibly experiencing 'outstanding successes' in this use of the pyramid form.

The technique is fairly simple, but does involve a fair amount of occult training. The first step is to order a small cardboard pyramid which is packaged with a pad of triangular sheets of paper. These sheets come in four colours: blue, for healing; green, for love; orange, for mental clarity; and yellow, for intuition.

The experimenter then chooses a coloured triangle most suited to his or her need, and writes a statement of a particular goal, or a request for the solution to a specific problem on that sheet. For example, should you wish to hasten the healing of a broken bone, you would write your request on a blue piece of paper; if you wanted to heal a lovers' quarrel, you would instead choose a green sheet.

The instructions stress that the request be worded as plainly and specifically as possible. If your thoughts are vague or confused, the experimenter is told, wait before writing your request. Later your thought will clarify itself and you will be able to write down exactly what it is you wish.

The experimenter then holds the paper between his or her palms and repeats a specific chant – apparently provided by the organization – twice. The apex of the triangle is then folded down to the base and the bottom folded up, so that the paper ends up folded into thirds. Next, the folded triangle is placed on the base of the pyramid, with the base aligned in a north-south direction and the written 'thought-form' on the bottom. The palms of the hands are then placed above the coloured paper and the chant is repeated again. The pyramid structure is then appropriately aligned over the base and the thought-form incubation period has begun.

Apparently, it takes three to nine days for the thought-form to complete its 'gestation period'. During that time the process is aided by chanting and feeding the thought-form by focusing on it mentally through the north side of the pyramid once every day.

When the experimenter feels that the thought-form has incubated long enough, he or she removes the pyramid from its base and picks up the paper with the thought-form written on it. The paper is then unfolded. A lower corner of the paper is grasped and the triangle is then set on fire. Once the flame has completely devoured the paper, the ashes are thrown into a fireproof receptacle which has been kept at hand throughout the proceedings.

The burning procedure is accomplished so that the thought-form can be released. It is compared to the fledgling's leaving the nest — once it is sufficiently mature it must be free to accomplish its purpose. Having completely liberated the thought-form (not a single shred of paper should remain) the experimenter then awaits the fulfilment of his or her request, knowing that the fire, the most powerful of the four holy elements, has released a fully-charged thought-form which will soon be translated into a reality.

As complex and bizarre as this procedure sounds, from all over the world, members of this organization have reported that their incubator pyramids have satisfied their requests — in the form of new jobs or business ventures, money and jewellery — among other things. Whether or not the requests which brought their receptors these material objects were of a religious nature, those who believe that their prayers were fulfilled are not complaining.

To further their research, E.S.P. Laboratory has constructed, at its Los Angeles headquarters, two life-size (six and eight feet high) pyramids. They have, one spokesman claims, discovered that the pyramid shape has numerous energy centres, called *chakras*, which are much like the centres in the human body. They also claim that they have discovered that the pyramid is relative to the human body in the same way that the key of E-flat (the pyramid) is relative to the key of C (the body).

More than 80 per cent of the experimental participants claimed that they could pinpoint definite energy centres inside the pyramids. Of these people, almost all noticed that the energy was of a higher frequency in the upper portions of both the six- and the eight-foot pyramids. An equally high percentage of persons noted that in the lower portions they felt a mildly warm and soothing feeling.

Another interesting observation made by many of the participants in these experiments was when they raised their hands into the apex, they experienced a pricking sensation, as if tiny needles were being stuck into the extremity.

The experimenters also reported that there are some spots in the pyramid which are not beneficial – for example, individuals who stood or sat in one particular spot inside the pyramid experienced headaches within a very short period of time.

Allegedly, the most beneficient energies inside the pyramid are focused within the so-called heart centre. This is the spot which is probably the 'safest' for the incubation of thought-forms. However, it has been suggested that different thought-forms might best be incubated at different spots in order for the person inside the pyramid to receive the energy most advantageous in fulfilling the specific thought-form.

States director Al Manning, '... this part of our project has great promise, but we must await further experimentation before commenting on its practical value.'

In another experiment Manning invited an unnamed television producer, and David St Clair, author of *The Psychic World of California*, to spend approximately twelve minutes inside the six-foot pyramid. The three men stood inside the structure, talked, then stepped outside. As they left the pyramid, both the producer and St Clair mentioned that they felt slightly 'woozy'. The next day St Clair phoned Manning and told him that when he got home the night before he had had to cancel a cocktail party because he was too sleepy to attend. He reported that he had fallen asleep around 6.30 p.m. and woke up feeling fantastically well. 'That Pyramid,' he said, 'really cleaned out my aura.'

The organization claims that they have also had excellent results with experimental attempts to use the pyramid to relieve migraine-type headaches.

Pyramid Power for Healing and Meditation

Many other claims have been made as to the healing properties of pyramids and many attempts have been made to explain these properties. One theory is that the pyramid focuses and intensifies unidentifiable energies to the extent that healing is possible. Another theory is that the atmosphere inside the pyramid stimulates an acceleration of enzyme action which accounts for the effects of mummification, preservation and possibly even the intensity of meditation. This explanation has lead one physician to suggest that the pyramid might be useful in the treatment of intractable oedema and even possibly as an aid to organ regeneration. This leads to the speculation that in the near future, hospitals will store vital organs for transplant purposes in pyramid-shaped containers.

One amateur pyramid researcher in Illinois suggests that the pyramid might be useful in the healing, or alleviation, of arthritis or rheumatism. She advises the sufferer to place the hand directly under the apex of a miniature pyramid, with the palm either up or down. Within seconds a tingling sensation will be felt in the hand, caused by a powerful vortex of energies spiraling within the pyramid. She claims that in order to 'fully charge' the hand, levitation of the extremity must take place inside the pyramid. Ostensibly, after approximately seven minutes inside the pyramid, the hand will begin to hover of its own volition. The hand is then fully charged and may be removed from the pyramid. Possibly, in the process of levitation, the hand has risen to the one-third level, where the sharpening and preserving powers act as an healing charge.

Many persons have recently acquired pyramid tents which they use for meditational purposes. These people claim they experience a range of feelings from calmness to extreme euphoria during their meditation sessions. The most common syndrome seems to begin with a relaxation of the body, then a shutting out of unnecessary external stimuli and irrelevant thoughts and a final achievement of an altered state of consciousness which allows the individual to concentrate on deeper inner levels.

A great number of people who use meditation pyramids on a regular basis report that they have experienced a definite loss of worry and tension. Others claim that they have attained a heightened charge of psychic energy, increased memory recall, views of past incarnations, visions, dreams, indescribably beautiful colours, forms, symbols, or music 'from the spheres'. Still others report that they hear the sound of *om* (*ahm*) a mantra of the universal 'I' when inside the pyramid, and some claim to receive wisdom and insights from higher planes. There are reports of experiences of precognition, interplanetary travel, telepathic communications, answers to prayers, and overall revitalization of the entire being. Since these astounding assertions have not been recorded under control conditions they can only be considered hearsay. However, it may be possible to use some of the brain wave recording technology to substantiate or refute at least some of these metaphysical claims.

Pyramid meditators suggest that the best results are achieved by sitting upright with the upper *chakras* (the force-centres of energy within) located at approximately one-third up from the pyramid base, directly under the apex.

Powers of Preservation

Another of the pyramid's mysterious energies is that of preservation. In *La Pyramide de Chéops a-t-elle livré son secret*? Ferrand Ibek says that the form of the Cheops' pyramid aided the mummification process inside the King's Chamber, where the body would dehydrate with virtually no signs of decay.

The ancient Egyptians prepared a body for mummification by pulling the viscera through the anus. The brains were removed by some suction process through the nasal passages. This prevented any damage to the shell of the body, thus enabling the spirit to return to an intact receptacle. Then, according to Egyptologists, the body would be soaked in a brine mixture for approximately a month, and plugs, usually perfumed with an onion scent, were placed in the ears, nostrils and other orifices. The entire body would then be wrapped in cloth in preparation for interment in the sarcophagus.

As far as can be determined, mummification rites were, at first, applied only to the Pharaohs. Then, as the religious age of Egypt became decadent, the nobility began to have themselves mummified. Eventually, the practice became quite widespread and the requirements for mummification became so lax that anyone who could afford the cost of the process was allowed to undergo it. So great did the vogue become that at one time even animals were mummified.

The mummification process is interpreted by Egyptologists as signifying the ability of the *Ka*, or the soul, of the deceased to regain entrance to this earth. If this hypothesis is accepted, it becomes obvious that mummification was necessary to preserve as completely as possible the body shell of the Pharaoh in order for his spirit to return properly.

However, an opposite, but equally likely interpretation, can be applied to the purpose of mummification. According to many mystics, the mummification process is actually an effective preventive measure *against* reincarnation. This seems plausible when it is understood that reincarnation was considered necessary for imperfect souls. For example an adept who had failed to pass any of the initiation rites would have to come back to earth rather than go on to eternal life. In this context, it would have been natural for the Pharaoh, considered 'the perfect one', to have his body mummified so that even if his spirit were the slightest bit unbalanced, it could not return to its former shell.

Still another theory is propounded by Manly P. Hall, who suggests that the body of the adept was mummified for the sole purpose of serving as a talisman to indicate that the spirit had an existence on earth. The major purpose, then, of the mummification of the Pharaoh would be as a medium through which his survivors could communicate with him.

An interesting parallel to the talisman theory can be found in a Peruvian ritual which required the population to mass in the sacred square of Cuzco on high holy days to witness the display of the mummies of past emperors of Inca civilizations. This showing of the mummies strengthened the belief of the masses in the structure of the ruling class. Even today, in many countries around the world, the Catholic and Orthodox churches display mummified parts of former saints on holy days or saints' days.

It is interesting to note that in the late 1700s and early 1800s, mummy flesh was used as a medicine. This flesh was mistaken for a drug called pitch or Persian moma, which healed small cuts and bruises. Mummy flesh was to be found in the stock of most European pharmacists and was strongly believed to have the powers to knit fractured bones immediately and to be beneficial for every type of internal disorder.

Apparently, the first person to discover the ability of the Great Pyramid to aid the mummification process was Antoine Bovis (see page 120), who visited the Pyramid sometime during the 1900s. In *Psychic Discoveries Behind the Iron Curtain*, Sheila Ostrander and Lynn Schroeder claim that they were told by Czechoslovakian scientists that Bovis, while walking around inside the King's Chamber, found seemingly preserved cats and other small animals which had apparently wandered into the Pyramid and died of starvation. Bovis thought that perhaps the shape of the Pyramid might have been responsible for the dehydrated state of these animals, which showed no signs of decay. Upon his return from Egypt, he decided to construct a model of the Pyramid with a base about 3 feet square. Since the King's Chamber is approximately one-third of the height of the Pyramid from the base, he experimented with placing specimens (dead cats) one-third of the way towards the apex from the base. Seemingly, his experiments were successful, because he concluded that there was something about the Pyramid's shape which prevented decay and caused rapid mummification.

Ostrander and Schroeder further deal with the Pyramid's energies of dehydration in their chapter titled *Pyramid Power and the Riddle of the Razor Blade*, in which they reproduce a table showing dehydration rates of various objects. This table was compiled by a Jean Martial, and gives somewhat scientific credence to pyramid experimentation. However, the authors fail to list the source from which they obtained Monsieur Martial's table, and the only reference they cite regarding the experimentation of Monsieur Bovis is a Czechoslovakian popular magazine article – hardly an unimpeachable scientific source.

The accounts of Bovis' experiments have become very popular and have appeared in many newspaper and magazine articles. Fortunately, we have the original source of these accounts recorded in Chapter 8.

Still another inexplicable property of the pyramid might be found in accounts of rooms in pyramids built from the Fifth and Sixth Dynasties on, which have painted figures on their walls. The mystery here concerns the light source used to illuminate these windowless chambers, since lack of carbon smudges indicates that torches were not utilized.

Static Electricity Accumulation

A more demonstrable property of the Pyramid is its seeming ability to act as an accumulator of static electricity.

In the *Secrets of the Great Pyramid*, Peter Tompkins relates that Sir W. Siemans, a British inventor, was standing on the apex of the Great Pyramid, when he noticed that whenever he raised his hands and spread his fingers, he heard a ringing sound. Further, whenever he raised just one finger, especially his index finger, he felt an irritating prickling sensation in that digit. (It is interesting to recall that similar prickling sensations were described by many of the participants in the E.S.P. lab experiments.)

Siemans, however, also noted that when he drank from the wine bottle he had brought along, he experienced a slight shock as the bottle touched his lips. The electrical activity intrigued Siemans so much that he took a wet newspaper and wrapped it around the bottle, converting it into a crude electrical accumulator called a Leyden jar.

When Siemans held the converted wine bottle high above his head, it accumulated tremendous amounts of static electricity, so much so that sparks began shooting from it. Accidentally, Siemans touched one of the guides with it. The guide received a tremendous shock, similar to that emitted by cattle prodders. Frightened by the shock, the guide fell. So terrified was he, that he fled down the side of the Pyramid.

This account (which is unsubstantiated, since Tompkins does not cite any reference source for it) is somewhat reminiscent of the biblical tale (Exodus, chapters 26 and 27; Second Samuel, chapter 6) of the Ark of the Covenant which Moses built with the help of the people of Israel. Many researchers today believe that the Ark was, in actuality, a Leyden jar in which the accumulation of electricity was so great that the charge it produced was enough to kill a person with a heart condition. Such a heart condition, they reason, could have been responsible for the death of Uzzah when he touched the Ark.

Some physicists believe that the Pyramid is not only an accumulator of energies, but also a modifier of these same energies. We know that any object within which energy vibrates is capable of acting as a resonating cavity. We also know that the energy is focused at a certain point within the object, whether it is hollow or solid. Thus we can conjecture that the pyramid may act as a huge resonating cavity which is able to focus energies of the cosmos like a giant lens. This focused energy would affect the molecules or crystals of any object in the path of the beam of focused energy. Some even equate it to an invisible Laser beam, having a different frequency and strength of affect.

Negative Effects

We find it particularly interesting that so far, very few reports of negative effects have been circulated about the pyramid. Unlike virtually all other occult paraphernalia, such as ouija boards and pendulums, the pyramid seems to have powers which are almost always either beneficial or neutral. Of course, some mystics complain that when they spend a great deal of time inside of a pyramid for meditational purposes, they actually received 'too much energy', or feel 'overcharged'. This, of course, would be the fault of the meditator, for not controlling his use of the pyramid, and not the fault of the pyramid itself.

The only report of truly negative effects we have heard to date is that of E.S.P. laboratory's experimentors who claim that standing in a specific portion of a large pyramid gave them a headache in short order.

Although the energies of the pyramid may, as yet, be inexplicable, there are some energies inside and surrounding the pyramid which are most certainly measurable. Through the use of radiesthesia, or dowsing rods, researchers have been able to show that there is an helical vortex of energy emanating from the apex of the pyramid which actually expands in diameter as it rises higher and higher. Using small cardboard pyramids only 4 inches high, dowsers have demonstrated that this vortex can reach a height of nearly 8 feet over the apex, and expand to a diameter of almost 6 feet. In a controlled experiment to demonstrate the existence of this vortex of energy, one miniature pyramid was placed underneath one of three identical cardboard boxes. The dowser, not knowing which box concealed the pyramid, then tested each one with his rod. The rod reacted only over the box with the pyramid.

Application of Pyramid Energies

Of all the energies of the pyramid, perhaps the best-known is its mysterious ability to keep razor blades sharp.

This ability was first brought to the attention of the public by Karl Drbal, a Czechoslovakian researcher, who has been experimenting with pyramid shapes since the early 1940s. During the 1950s, in Prague, he received patent number 91304 on a pyramid which he used to prolong the longevity of razor blades. Although some scientists in various parts of the world have been cognizant of the Drbal patent, it was not until the publication of *Psychic Discoveries Behind the Iron Curtain*, that the general public became aware of Drbal's claim for the energies of pyramid shapes. Since the inception of this mass recognition, numerous research studies have been conducted throughout the world to support or validate these claims. Although there is no clear consensus in the scientific community as to the effectiveness of the pyramid in maintaining the sharpness of razor blades, hundreds of undocumented experiments have been performed by laymen which support the sharpening ability of the pyramid.

Shortly after the Czechoslovakian razor sharpener was popularized by Ostrander and Schroeder, engineer Karl Drbal authorized a New York writer and researcher to begin distribution of the pyramid throughout the United States. Within three years, the company the writer formed to distribute the pyramid has become so successful that it now internationally distributes the pyramids.

Apparently convinced that the much-touted *Flower Power* of the '60s is being replaced, in this decade, by Pyramid Power, many commercial firms have jumped on this seemingly lucrative bandwagon. One firm in Michigan offers a standard cardboard pyramid and a not-so-standard one which, when one peers through its apex, offers an entertaining variety of figures, forms and scenes, ostensibly visions from the past. This same company also sells a shaving cream bomb to be used in conjunction with the razor blade to be stored in the pyramid.

A California firm also offers a model pyramid, but its main item is a large pyramid, made of plastic sheeting, which resembles a translucent Cub Scouts' pup tent. This pyramid is sold and used primarily for meditation purposes, although many rejuvenating effects have been attributed to it. Still another product sold by this firm is a plate, ostensibly 'charged' inside a pyramid, which is supposed to alter the taste of foods, tobacco and liquor. The manufacturers suggest that one of the possible uses of this plate is to aid in the growth of ordinary house plants. Allegedly, water which is left for several hours a day on this plate, and then poured over plants, will help your greenery flourish.

Not all pyramid distributors are aiming at a mystical or occult market. A leading mail order firm of scientific supplies and equipment has two types of pyramids listed in its latest catalogue – a clear plastic model and a cardboard model. While this company does not make any claims for the energies of the pyramid, they do offer it as an item which might be of interest to students searching for experimental subjects for science fair projects.

While we were not, at this time, able to ascertain how well these distribution companies are doing financially, we can state with conviction that the pyramid is definitely a saleable item, and the purchasers are using their miniature pyramids for everything from thought-form incubators to experimental devices to razor blade containers. One of the most far-out uses of a table model pyramid which has come to our attention is as a storage place for lottery tickets. The reports of people winning with pyramid-stored lottery tickets are numerous. This does not necessarily mean that the pyramid actually has the power to help the owners of the tickets to win lotteries. It could merely mean that the people who placed lottery tickets inside pyramids, and lost, are keeping this information to themselves.

Other reports, even more difficult to substantiate, come from people who claim that when they placed a model pyramid near their beds or chairs, after several nights of sleep, or several days of sitting near the pyramid, a specific pain or symptom of illness either disappeared or was greatly alleviated.

Although movie actress Gloria Swanson does not claim to have been healed or cured by pyramid energy, she was quoted by *Time Magazine* (October 8, 1973) as stating that sleeping with a miniature pyramid under her bed made 'every cell in my body tingly'.

Another Hollywood star who is pro-pyramid is James Coburn, who, according to the *National Enquirer* of 13 January 1974, says, 'I firmly believe in pyramid power. I crawl inside my pyramid tent, sit in a yoga position, and does it work! It gives off a definite feeling and sensation. It creates an atmosphere ... that makes it easier to meditate. It closes out all interference. I meditate in there every day, between fifteen minutes to an hour.'

Pyramid tents are now being used for activities which range from sleep to rigorous exercise. Some people who have used the pyramid for meditational purposes claim they have reached better and deeper levels of meditation when they were inside. Other people who have slept in pyramids claim that they could not do so for more than three nights in a row, because they were so energized that they could not cope with the dynamo effects they experienced. The energy experienced by these persons is so great that it *cannot* be explained, as some authorities have attempted to do, by ascribing it to the placebo effect, the phenomenon whereby an individual responds, not to an actual occurrence or stimulus, but to the suggestion of such an occurrence or stimulus.

Pyramidal Headgear

The man primarily responsible for the phenomenal interest in miniature pyramids, Karl Drbal, might yet start a new craze — *pyramid hats*. Drbal, who began to wonder why the traditional witches' and sorcerers' hats were always depicted as being cone-shaped, ran a few experiments with hats in the shape of pyramids. One New York researcher asserts that after wearing the pyramid hat for a short time a tremendous influx of spiraling energy could be felt coming down through the tip of the hat. 'Apparently,' he said, 'the pyramid acts like a kind of cosmic antenna turning into sources of energy of vaster intensity and then focusing it into its centre.'

Others who have worn them claim that these pyramid hats definitely relieve headaches.

The history of conical hats used for religious and mystical purpose is a long one. It can actually, according to one psychic, be traced back to the Egyptian priests who wore pyramid hats when they were trying to contact their sun god, Ra. It has been speculated that these hats actually focused electromagnetic energy from the sun or from some higher metaphysical plane. If this reason is correct, the wearers of these hats would have been the possessors of special energies and would therefore naturally have been accorded the awe and respect of the masses.

J. Forlong, in *Rivers of Life*, also claims that cone hats were originally connected with solar worship. They later came to denote professional status and were worn, not only by sorcerers, but by priests and kings. These hats were always decorated to clearly identify the sect and rank (of nobility) of the wearer. Forlong notes that the common priest's hat was a cone of very considerable dimensions. Derivative of this conical headgear, says Forlong, was the early musician's hat – shaped like a fish with its tail uppermost.

One researcher speculates that the so-called dunce hat, also traditionally cone-shaped, was originally used as a functional device for 'tuning a person back into his basic centre'. He argues that children who misbehave do so because they have 'lost (there) centre of balance'. By sitting in a corner, wearing a cone-shaped hat, they will become 'returned'. 'Notice,' he says, '(that) the child usually faces into the corner so that he is not distracted by activity in the class. All of his energy must be centred more in himself.'

One New York medium apparently does not need a conical hat to receive the benefit of the energies of the geometric shape. In *Seth Materials*, Jane Roberts writes that under certain conditions, 'I got the feeling that a cone came down just over my head. I didn't think that an actual physical cone was there, but the idea of shape was definite. The wide end was about the size of my head, with the narrow part on top *like a pyramid*. (Emphasis added by authors.)

In this chapter we have dealt primarily with the metaphysical aspects of pyramid experimentation. In the following chapters, we will inform you of some of the more pragmatic aspects of pyramid research, given you instructions for building your own pyramid, and offer suggestions for carrying out your own experiments.

10

Pyramid Research

A great deal of attention has focused on the reports which ascribe unusual properties to scale models of the Pyramid. Such has been the interest in these reports that a central data pool for pyramid research was established in Washington, D.C. in late 1973 by Mankind Research Unlimited, Inc.

Dr Boris Vern, Director of this Pyramid Research Project, conducted pilot experiments using plastic pyramids 10 inches high, and plastic cubes of equal volume. These experiments yielded the following results: raw eggs in dishes placed under pyramids hardened and dried in less than three weeks time. Various molds placed on these eggs would not grow. In contrast to this, control eggs remained moist and served as receptive media to enhance mold growth. These control eggs seem to undergo certain deformations when placed under pyramids after two weeks' exposure to control space.

In a letter to us, Dr Vern stated: 'Working on the assumption that the dehydration effect might be due to relative differences in water evaporation and perhaps on the presence of relatively different areas of blotter paper (used as bases for the structures), the following was done:

A weighed quantity of water was placed under each structure in a plastic dish. Rates of evaporation were determined by daily weighings. This procedure was carried out using three different bases: (1) blotter paper, (2) aluminium foil, and (3) structures elevated 4cm above table level to allow for free air exchange. Light and temperature were identical in all three cases.

I include three graphs (Figures 26, 27 and 28) showing rates of evaporation for the above 3 conditions. It can be seen that in Figures 26 and 27 rates were more rapid under pyramids than under cubes; however, the rates become identical in Figure 28. It is possible that differences in air currents exist in different parts of the experimental

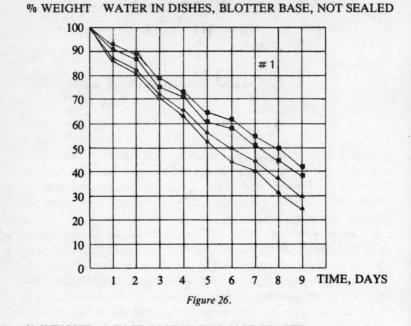

Figure 26.

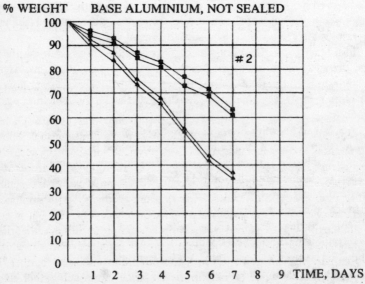

Figure 27.

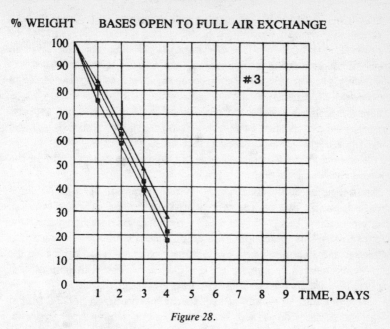

% WEIGHT   BASES OPEN TO FULL AIR EXCHANGE

Figure 28.

room. To test for this additional variable, the bases of the structures will be sealed with plastic.'

Unfortunately, at the time of publication, 'the results of this critical part of the experiment' had not yet been made available to us.

Added Dr Vern, 'The paucity of results at this time precludes statistical analysis, which must await repeated testing.'

Researchers have conclusively demonstrated that objects placed inside pyramid shapes are acted upon by unusual properties. These properties are independent of known physical variables because the physical variables could not, by themselves, reproduce the properties. Therefore, experimenters are faced with a physical phenomenon foreign to accepted concepts of physics and chemistry, a phenomenon which, one might assume, is a product of physical forces, but is not capable of being explained by known physical properties and theories. They are thus compelled to choose a proper perspective within which to explore this phenomenon in a thorough and unbiased manner. It certainly seems wiser to pursue the empirical approach rather than blindly accept the preconceived postulates concerning physical principles. One proof of the wisdom of this approach is that several high school students, in the United States, using the empirical method of research have produced prize-winning (including the first prize in several instances) science fair projects centring around pyramids.

Many phenomena have been repeatedly observed in pyramids. The dehydration aspects of the energies within the pyramids are more commonly the subject of experimentation than any other aspects. Pyramidal dehydration of flowers, fruits, vegetables, animals, fish and insects is fairly well established as fact.

The late Verne Cameron, ran some impressive experiments on the preservative powers of the pyramid.

First, he carefully constructed a small pyramid. Then he obtained approximately two ounces of raw pork, one ounce of which was fat. After placing the pork inside the pyramid, he in turn placed the pyramid in his bathroom. Cameron had deliberately chosen the hottest and steamiest room in the house – the one room subject to the greatest changes in temperature and humidity. The bathroom atmosphere is definitely not conducive to the preservation of food.

Keeping careful watch on his experiment, Cameron noticed that at the end of three days there was a faint odour coming from the pork, apperently the first signs of decay setting in. But, according to Cameron, six days later the smell had vanished and the piece of raw pork was completely mumified. Even more astounding is his claim that after several months of storage inside the bathroom-situated pyramid, the pork was perfectly edible.

In another experiment Cameron placed a large chunk of watermelon inside the pyramid and, placed it, once again, in his bathroom. In a few days the watermelon had dried down to apricot size. But it, too, remained perfectly edible. Said Cameron, 'it was still sweet and good'.

Being a dedicated scientist, Cameron naturally wondered what was causing these unlikely phenomena. To try to find out, he used an aurameter, a device he had invented, which measures the force-field aura of objects. He asserted that he measured a column of energy extending from the apex of the pyramid to the height of the ceiling. He also reported that a small pyramid is like the capstone of a larger invisible pyramid-field that reaches along imaginary lines of force from the base of the 'capstone' to the floor. Cameron further claimed that once the pyramid was removed from a spot on which it had stood, the charge sometimes remained for several days or even weeks.

Simple Experiments

To dehydrate any specimen, place it on a platform or directly on the base with its longest axis aligned in the north-south direction. The specimens need not be centred, that is, not placed directly under the apex, although there certainly seems to be validity in centring it. The time required for the dehydration period varies in accordance with the physical size and moisture content of the specimen. Periodic inspection of the specimen may be made during the dehydration process. Care must be taken not to damage the specimen while inspecting it; also, it must be replaced exactly in the position it was in before it was handled. Once total dehydration is achieved the object can be removed from the pyramid and put on display.

To experiment with milk, or any other desired fluid, place the liquid in a small, shallow, non-metallic dish. Place a control dish outside the pyramid with the same quantity of milk. After several days both containers of milk with turn sour, but the one in the pyramid will not be curdled.

Shrinking and/or shrivelling of experimental specimens depends on the ratio of moisture to fibre content. The higher the moisture content, the more shrunken and misshapen the specimen, as in the case of daffodils, which have a high moisture/low fibre content ratio. Roses, on the other hand, have a low moisture/high fibre content ratio and dehydrate almost perfectly inside the pyramids, with virtually no signs of shrivelling or shrinking.

In carrying out a meaningful research experiment involving the dehydration process, you should employ the following control procedures:

1. Weigh the specimen before placing it in the pyramid; reweigh it every day thereafter, until total dehydration is accomplished, to determine the dehydration rate for the specific specimen.

2. Set up other containers, such as a cardboard box, a metal box, a tin can, etc., with and without covers. Each of these containers should have a volume equal to that of the pyramid. In each of these control containers place a specimen as nearly identical as possible to the specimen in the pyramid. These specimens should also be weighed each day, at the same time as the specimen inside the pyramid. After weighing, realign every specimen in its exact previous position.

3. Place still another identical specimen on a flat surface in the open air. This, too, should be weighed each day along with the other specimens.

4. Start a log and record in it the following information: composition, dimensions and age of specimens at the beginning of the experiment; composition, dimensions, shape and volume of each container. On each subsequent day, weigh all the specimens and visually check them for signs of discolouration, firmness and decay. Enter any pertinent information of this type in the log, dating it appropriately.

It is important to keep in mind that most commercially available food stuffs, both prepared and raw, are treated with chemical preservatives which may affect the dehydration rate, thus invalidating your experiment. Therefore it is wisest, when experimenting with foodstuffs, to use only those which are preservative free or, in the case of fruit and vegetables, organically grown.

Having compared the dehydration process which occurs within the pyramid to that which takes place in other containers, you might then wish to experiment with the differences in the dehydration process which occur at various height levels within the pyramid itself. For instance, you might obtain or build several identical pyramids and place inside them identical specimens, altering only the height from the base at which the specimen is placed, e.g., one specimen might be placed directly on the base, another at the 1/6 level, and still others at the 1/5, 1/4, 1/3 and 1/2 levels. The height of the level is measured up from the base, i.e., the 1/3 level of a 6-inch pyramid is 2 inches above the base.

In various European countries, e.g., Yugoslavia, Italy and France, milk and yogurt are now packaged in pyramid-shaped cartons. Apparently, this type of packaging retards the spoilage process, enabling consumers to retain these products for a much longer period of time than they could when the same products were packaged in conventional containers. Although there is no data to support the claim of prolonged shelf life due to pyramidal packaging, we do know that the pyramid shape acts as a preservative, nor can we think of any other rationale for the manufacturers' having incurred the enormous expenses involved in changing the packaging of these products. Also, it hardly seems possible that mere coincidence was responsible for the decision of American manufacturers to package cream for restaurants in tiny pyramid-shaped packets. These packets are kept under coffee shop counters all day long without refrigeration and have an unusually long shelf life. It is very likely that the pyramid shape is responsible for the longevity of the cream, although it is also possible that the cream lasts simply because spoilage-retardent preservatives have been added to it. In this context, however, it does seem significant that in Czarist Russia the military troops allegedly received their meat rations in pyramid-shaped containers, designed precisely for the purpose of preservation.

In recent times, more and more people have begun to use pyramid-shaped storage containers for dried grain and other food stuffs, claiming that products stored in this manner have a fresher taste than the same products stored in conventionally shaped containers. Try storing rice, dried beans, dried fruits, condiments or even candy, cookies, etc., in pyramid-shaped containers. You can expect a definite improvement in the taste of these items. In addition, you should find that these containers are bug-free, in the summer months, whereas small insects seem to proliferate in conventional containers during hot, humid weather.

It had been suggested that coffee, when stored in a pyramid, has a less bitter taste. There are also claims that cigars, cigarettes and pipe tobacco will become milder if you keep them in a pyramid. Supposedly, pyramid storage mellows whisky and ages beer. And there are even claims that strong perfumes, left inside pyramids, have been altered to subtler fragrances.

In its information sheet, mailed to pyramid purchasers, one California firm suggests that the miniature pyramid can be used for making cottage cheese or pot cheese. They instruct you to place a glass of fresh, unpasteurized, whole milk in your pyramid, directly under the apex. They then tell you to align the pyramid along the north-south axis and leave the milk inside it for a period of three to five weeks. Periodic checks of the glass should show that the milk is beginning to curdle and a crust starting to form on top. Do not disturb this crust until the incubation period has ended. This will occur when the milk in the glass has taken on, to your satisfaction, the appearance of pot cheese or cottage cheese. You can then remove the glass from the pyramid, scrape off the crust, and eat your home-made cheese.

In Chapter 7, we discussed E.S.P. laboratory's experiments with using pyramids to incubate 'thought-forms'.

Should you wish to use your own miniature pyramid as a thought-form incubator, simply write your request or prayer, as simply and specifically as possible, on a regular sheet of paper and fold it in half. Then, hold the paper between your hands as a focal point for building a force field, concentrate totally on the written thought-form and, at the same time, charge the paper with love and tenderness. Finally, place it inside your pyramid, making sure that both the paper and the pyramid itself are properly aligned along a north-south axis.

Unfortunately, we cannot provide you with the appropriate chant, but you can mentally focus on the thought-form once a day, through the north side of the pyramid.

As discussed in Chapters 8 and 9, pyramids can be used to maintain the sharpness of both single- and double-edged razor blades, household knives and scissors. There are even reports of the usage of pyramids to prolong the amount of time an *electric razor head* will remain sharp.

Extremely dull razor blades and other cutting implements can actually be sharpened by housing them in pyramids, but this process is a fairly lengthy one — the instrument in question must remain unmoved inside a pyramid for at least four months.

Razor Blade Experiment
To conduct your own experiment to determine whether or not the

RAZOR BLADE IN PYRAMID

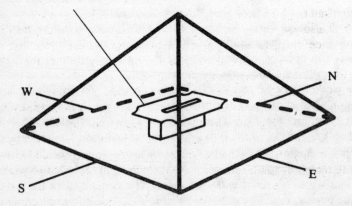

Figure 29.

pyramid actually does prolong the sharpness of a razor blade you will need only a pyramid, a blade and a considerable amount of patience.

Place a brand new razor blade inside your pyramid. For optimum results, place it flat on the $\frac{1}{3}$ level and with its cutting edges aligned facing east-west. Allow the blade to remain in the pyramid for at least one full week. It may then be used for periodic or daily shaving. As long as the blade is returned to the pyramid after each shave, and positioned exactly as it was during the seven-day conditioning period, it should retain its sharpness. For the first forty to sixty days of use, the subjective quality of the shaves will probably fluctuate a great deal. However, after this initial period, the quality will stabilize and will normally remain constant for at least two hundred shaves more (see Figure 29).

Since 1970, a number of new ways to utilize the powers of the pyramids have developed in such diverse fields as horticulture, electronics and biochemistry. Some of the ideas which have evolved are simple, practical and easily affected for daily use.

Pyramids and Horticulture
Horticulturists have found that seeds which were placed inside a pyramid before planting germinated more quickly and produced a stronger, healthier plant in a shorter period of time than did seeds which had not been processed in a pyramid.

It is also interesting to note that any horticulturist whose field of experience is in the growing of grapevines will inform you that to insure a good, tasty crop of grapes, it is necessary to have the vines growing or climbing in a north-south direction.

Large pyramids are increasingly being used as hot houses and sanitoriums to maintain the life of plants during their dormant cycles and to rehabilitate plants which no longer seem to be thriving.

To perform your own horticultural experiment, simply buy a package of seeds. Place half of the seeds inside your pyramid in rows along the north-south axis and leave them there for at least two weeks. Then remove the seeds and plant them. As a control, plant the rest of the seeds under identical conditions; carefully identify each group of seeds. By observing the growth rate of each batch of seeds, you will be able to draw your own conclusions as to the efficacy of the pyramid in aiding seed germination.

Two particularly practical uses for pyramids concern ordinary house plants. One way in which your plants can be benefitted by the pyramid is to use it as a storage container for the water you use watering your window-sill garden. Place ordinary tap water inside a pyramid for at least a week before you use it to water your plants. You will probably find that it will stimulate plant growth, acting much like a fertilizer. Many reports of rapid increase in floral propagation, and our own experimentation, suggest that water housed within a pyramid actually undergoes a change, as yet undetectable in chemical analysis, which not only aids plant growth, but in fact helps seeds to germinate more quickly than they would when watered naturally, and actually produces a healthier seedling.

The other way in which your pyramid can help your plants is by using it to root cuttings. It appears that cuttings placed in pyramids to root do so much more quickly than under ordinary conditions. Also, the rate of loss of pyramid-rooted cuttings is less than that of cuttings rooted in water or soil outside the pyramid. To test the effectiveness of this method of rooting, simply place a cutting in a container of water. Then place the container inside the pyramid. Within a shorter period of time than it would normally take, the cutting will have a substantial root system. You can then remove it from the pyramid and pot it immediately. Watering it with pyramid-stored water should further insure the healthy growth of your cutting.

In the field of electronics, technologists have discovered that when they tuned an AM radio in between stations and fed the antenna wire an inch or two through the apex of a model pyramid from the outside, and then suspended the pyramid over another pyramid, unusual static issued from the radio's speaker. Moving the suspended pyramid away from the base pyramid resulted in reduction of the volume of the static to the point where it could no longer be heard.

Discovery of the fact that electronic signals issue from pyramids has led some enterprising persons to conduct experiments which have produced surprisingly practical results. Using an aluminium pyramid, they have created an antenna for TV and FM radio reception. This is accomplished by attaching each wire from the TV or radio antenna to an aluminium pyramid with a screw and hanging this complex above the television or radio.

Pendulums and Dowsing Rod

You can construct a pendulum from a small but heavy object, such as a ring or a coin, suspended from a thread of thin string about ten inches in length. The object you choose must be fairly heavy and as small as possible. A metal ball bearing is best; a door key is too large to be acceptable. Holding the pendulum in your hand, suspend it about one inch above the apex and about a foot to the left or right of the pyramid. Begin to move the pendulum *slowly* towards the pyramid. As it approaches the side or corner of the pyramid, and is about six inches from the apex, the pendulum will begin to be inexplicably prevented from reaching the apex, even though your hand is directly above or slightly past the apex. As a further test, suspend the weight about $\frac{1}{4}$ of an inch directly above the apex of the pyramid. Try to keep it motionless. You will probably find that this is practically impossible; in all likelihood the pendulum will swing away or move in a circular path around the apex.

To construct a dowsing rod, we suggest that you use a pair of metal coat hangers and straighten them out. Or use two metal rods, at least 1/16 of an inch in diameter and about 3 feet long. About 7 inches from one end of each rod, make a 90 degree bend. Each rod should now have a new length of about 29 inches and a 7-inch handle (see Figure 30). To operate these rods, grasp the handles gently in your

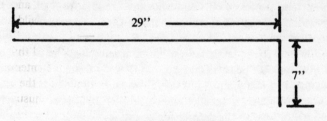

Figure 30. Dowsing Rod.

hands — do not squeeze them, since this would prevent the rods from swinging. Place your hands so that the rods are parallel to each other and pointing away from you.

With your arms extended at a comfortable level, walk towards the pyramid so that the rods will bracket the pyramid *above* the apex. As the tip of each rod approaches the apex, the rods will either begin to cross over each other, forming an 'X', or they will swing away from each other, one pointing to the right and the other pointing to the left.

The extent to which energy is radiated above the model pyramid can be determined by simply suspending the pendulum or the rods at increasingly greater heights above the apex until no effect is noticed.

The diameter of the energy vortex, or cone, can be determined by suspending either the pendulum or the rods above and slightly to the side of the apex of the pyramid. Note at what height and distance away from the apex your pendulum, or rods, first begin to react to the energy vortex. Now raise the instrument an inch and move it back from the pyramid to your original starting point. You should find that the higher above the apex the instrument is suspended, the greater the diameter of the area over which the effect of the energy vortex extends.

Although biochemical researchers have only recently begun to experiment with pyramids, some tentative findings have been reported (as discussed in the beginning of this chapter). Cultures, enzymes and bacteria seem to behave differently, based on their specific characteristics, inside pyramids than they do outside them. Researchers have also found, as have hundreds of lay experimenters, that mold and mildew does not seem to flourish very well inside a pyramidal environment.

It seems obvious that pyramids do contain some as yet unexplainable powers. Why then have many researchers, both amateur and professional, found negative results from their pyramid experiments? One reason is that many of these experiments have been conducted haphazardly, with improper materials, without proper controls and under less than optimum conditions. The effects of the pyramid may not be earthshaking, but they do seem to be of benefit to humankind in many small but useful ways. In order to best cull from the pyramid all of its benefits, the researcher must approach pyramid experiments with all the respect for scientific methods he or she would accord any conventional area of research.

11

Model Pyramid Construction

If you are interested in performing your own experiments and would like to build a pyramid to your own specifications, rather than purchasing a commercially prefabricated one, we offer herewith detailed instructions for three different methods of pyramid construction.

Apparently, the exact geometric construction of the pyramid is based on mathematics involving two irrational numbers. Irrational numbers are the result of fractions in decimal form which go on to infinity without repeating any set of numbers. The two irrational numbers are Pi and Phi, where Pi $(\pi) = 3.1415 \ldots$ and Phi $(\phi) = 1.618$ ... Phi is the number known as the Golden Section of the pyramid and is determined by the proportions incorporated by the pyramid. The pyramid base is a square, and the four sides are isoceles triangles. If we assign the value of 1.0 to half of the triangle base, the slant height (apothem) is Phi and the exact perpendicular height from the apex to the base is the square root of Phi. Therefore, Phi is an actuality equal to the area of each base. We leave the actual proof of this equation to those strongly knowledgeable in mathematics. Phi and Pi are related to each other by the approximate equation,

$$\pi = \frac{4}{\sqrt{\phi}}$$

Note that each face of the pyramid slants towards the apex at an angle of 51 degrees, 52 minutes and 10 seconds.

Choice of material seems to be very important in the construction of a model pyramid for experimental purposes. The construction materials should be homogeneous throughout. For example, compressed cardboard and not corrugated cardboard, solid wood as opposed to plywood, styrene plastic instead of styrofoam.

Method I

If your mechanical ability is somewhat limited because of inaccessibility of drafting tools, you may construct a pyramid by taking four sheets of cardboard. Using a ruler and a pencil, scribe out on the cardboard an isoceles triangle whose equal sides, S, are in the ratio to the base, B, of 1.051 to 1.0.

For example, if you wish to construct a pyramid approximately 8 inches high, you would need four pieces of cardboard 12 inches square. Place a ruler at each corner and draw in the lines where each ruler touches the other at $11\frac{1}{2}$ inches (see Figure 31).

An alternative method would be to use a large pair of compasses, with an opening of at least 12 inches. Set the compass to $11\frac{1}{2}$ inches and scribe an arc from the two bottom corners of the cardboard. The intersection represents the apex of the triangle. Draw the sides from this intersection marking to the bottom corners. Cut the triangles from the cardboard sheets and tape them together to form your pyramid.

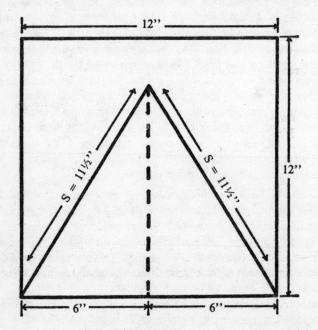

Figure 31.

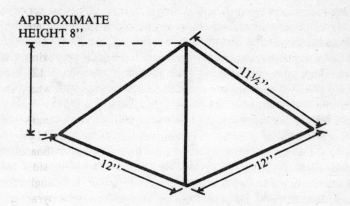

APPROXIMATE
HEIGHT 8"

11½"

12"

12"

Figure 32.

For intermediate or smaller sized pyramids, use the following table:

Base	Sides	Approximate Height
3 inches	2.85 inches	2 inches
6 inches	5.70 inches	4 inches
9 inches	8.55 inches	6 inches

1. Determine the desired height of the pyramid you wish to build.

2. Choose a number which, when multiplied by one of the numbers in the third column, will equal the desired height of the pyramid. For example, say you want your pyramid to be 8 inches high. Four inches when multiplied by two equal eight inches. Therefore, use the middle line of the table, the one in which the approximate height is 4 inches. Your multiplier is 2.

3. Now multiply each of the numbers in columns one and two (6 inches and 5.70 inches) by 2.

4. You know that a pyramid approximately 8 inches tall must have a base of 12 inches and sides of approximately 11½ inches (see Figure 32).

Method II

To construct a pyramid in one piece, take a pair of compasses and referring to the diagram (see Figure 33), draw a circle $5\frac{7}{8}$ inches in radius.

Draw a line from the centre to the outer point (a) and set the compass to 6 inches. From point (a) mark off one 6 inch length on the circle (b). From point (b) mark off another 6 inch point on the circle (c). Then from point (c) mark off another 6 inch length (d). Finally, from point (d) mark off the remaining 6 inches to point (e).

With a ruler, connect points (a) to (b), (b) to (c), (c) to (d), (d) to (e) and (e) to the centre. Score a line with a dull knife, from b, c, d to the centre (see Figure 33).

Cut along the pencil lines, fold on the scored lines and tape the edges together. This construction will yield a pyramid approximately 4 inches high, with a 6 inch square base.

If you want to make a circle several feet in diameter, you can construct a wooden trammel from a yardstick or a narrow slat slightly longer than the desired radius of the circle. At each end of the stick,

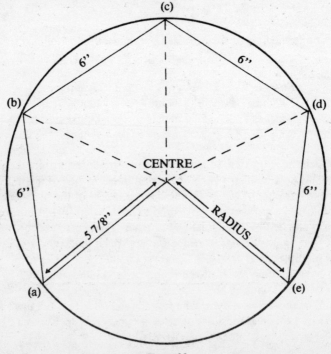

Figure 33.

drill a hole. The distance between the two holes should be equal to the radius of the circle. Insert a pencil in one hole, a nail in the other. Use the nail as the radius centre, or pivot point. To scribe the circle, use the trammel as you would a compass.

Method III

Accurately trace the following template (Figure 34).

Extend the sides, S, of the template to whatever size pyramid you desire. Triplicating this process will yield four triangles identical to the first method. The four triangular pieces will have to be taped together.

If you wish to be even more accurate, obtain a very precise protractor. Set the protractor to 61 degrees and draw the angles, extending the lines to whatever size you wish your pyramid to be.

Once you have constructed the pyramid, keep in mind the fact that your construction is not an accurate one; that the exact proportion or ratio will not be perfect and may affect the results of your experiments.

As an adequate control for having your pyramid slightly out of

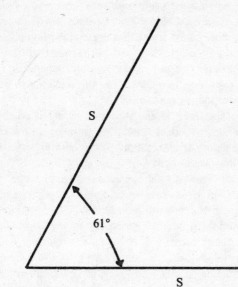

Figure 34.

proportion, we suggest that you place a mark towards the base on one of the faces, and keep this dot oriented to a cardinal point during the experiment.

At this point, you may wish to construct a base to support the pyramid and allow for easy relocation. Simply cut a square piece of cardboard 4 inches bigger than the base of the pyramid. For example, if you have constructed a pyramid with a 6 inch base, cut a piece of cardboard 10 inches square.

Most experiments can be carried out with a specimen placed directly on the base, but not necessarily in the centre. Apparently, experimental results are enhanced by elevating the specimen $\frac{1}{3}$ the height of the pyramid from the base. If you wish, you can construct your own platform from any material you prefer.

Worldwide experiments suggest that the forces responsible for the unusual properties are focused upon a point exactly at the $\frac{1}{3}$ level. Small or very thin specimens should be elevated on a platform to bring them as close to this level as possible. However, the total height of the platform plus the specimen should not go beyond the $\frac{1}{3}$ level.

Finally, each of the four faces should point in the direction of the four cardinal points; north, east, south and west. True north should be used for orientation purposes. However, magnetic north appears to work as well, and is more easily found. To determine magnetic north, a good quality compass should be used. True north differs from magnetic north by several degrees of declination, depending on the latitude where you live. You can determine the declination in your area by consulting your local almanac.

When placing the specimen in the pyramid, orient it so that the longest axis is in the direction of the north-south poles. In the case of specimens which are nearly round, simply place them in the centre of the pyramid so that they are directly below the apex.

One good way to ascertain if your pyramid is aligned properly is to place ordinary honey in a shallow rectangular dish and align the longest axis of the dish in a north-south direction. After a maximum of five days, if the pyramid is properly aligned, the honey should start to solidify and become tacky to the touch. When the pyramid is shifted slightly from proper alignment, the honey will, within twenty-four hours, once again become fluid. If, however, after the maximum five day period, the honey is still fluid, you will know that either the pyramid itself, or the honey container, or both, are slightly misaligned.

Of course the pyramid should be situated so that it will not be disturbed during your experiment. Also, the surrounding environment should be relatively constant in temperature and humidity. Since the process is theoretically based on cosmic, magnetic and other natural radiation energies, your experiment should not be conducted too closely to radios, television sets, or other high frequently or high voltage-producing devices.

We cannot stress too strongly that the primary factors required for successful pyramid experimentation are patience, precision, and scientific detachment. If your early experiment should prove unsuccessful, carefully analyze what you have done. Check to make sure that your pyramidal measurements are correct, that you have properly aligned both the pyramid and the object inside it, kept your specimen inside the pyramid for the specified minimum length of time and have observed the proper controls. Even if you have ascertained that you have complied with all of these requirements, do not give up. Repeat the experiment. There may be other factors at play which you, or we, have not considered and which, given time, can be alleviated or dispelled. In fact, should you be able to pinpoint a negative factor not previously noted by pyramid researchers, you may actually have discovered something of great importance to the science of pyramidology.

12

Enjoying the Fruits of Pyramid Energy

by
Joan Ann De Mattia

*Joan Ann De Mattia holds an A.B. degree from University College —
Rutgers, and an M.T. from the institute of Psychorientology, Laredo,
Texas. In addition to her career as a professional writer and editor, she
teaches Memory Training and Concentration and conducts weekly workshops in How to Develop Psychic Abilities. Ms De Mattia served as
Coordinator of the Western Hemisphere for the First International Con-
ference on Psychotronic Research in Prague in 1973 for which she wrote
a paper on Enhancing Creativity Through Altered States of Consciousness. At the Second ICPR in Monte Carlo in 1975 she presented a
paper on The Practical Applications of Orgone Energy, and she is the
inventor of an orgone energy collar. Ms De Mattia has been actively interested in pyramid energy since 1971 and here recounts her most curious
and fascinating experiences with pyramid power.*

About four years ago when I got my first pyramids from the Toth
Pyramid Company, N.Y.C., I tried to be as scientific as I could in
doing my experiments. I started out by placing a lovely yellow rose in
the centre of one little cardboard pyramid on a Chanel No. 5 box top
because it was precisely one-third the height of my pyramid. I placed
another yellow rose outside the pyramid on a piece of white paper as a
control specimen. Then I placed a third yellow rose in another
pyramid on a box top. All three were aligned on the true geographic
north-south axis.

On each of five successive days, I weighed both the 'pyramid rose'
and the 'outside rose' and made a note of the weight and colour. I left

the third rose undisturbed. By the fourth day the 'pyramid rose' appeared to be completely mummified. The colour had intensified, and it still had a slight scent of rose. The 'outside rose' had lost its scent, and the colour of the petals was somewhat faded. The flower was dehydrated but brittle, and the leaves broke off easily at the slightest touch, compared to the 'pyramid rose', which was dry and sturdy and still scented. The undisturbed rose was exquisitely beautiful; the colour was much more intense than when fresh; the scent was as strong as on day 1. The petals and leaves were dried but sturdy. Curiously, all three specimens lost the same amount of weight.

Next, I tried some crab apples, using the same procedure as with the roses: one crab apple inside a pyramid undisturbed, one outside for a control, and a third inside to be weighed and measured against the control. After three weeks of weighing and measuring, there was no appreciable difference in appearance or weight from day 1. When it became clear that it would take the crab apples a long, long time to mummify, I decided to leave the scientific experiments to the scientists and just have fun with my pyramids.

Then I did sliced mushrooms and sliced crab apples. They both take about 6 to 8 weeks depending on the size. We ate up all the mushrooms and most of the crab apple slices, but I still have some of the original sliced apples. I am sorry now that I gave away the whole crab apples, especially since they took about 3 months to mummify. The mushrooms tasted just like fresh ones, kept their colour, and looked a little wrinkled and dried. Every once in a while I sample a tiny piece of sliced apple. It is amazing that they still have a 'fresh apple' flavour and the skin is as colourful as it was on day 1. Only noticeable difference is that the sliced apples look dried out and slightly wrinkled.

The quickest and most useful items to mummify are herbs. I have done parsley, celery leaves, mint leaves, dill, and basil.* All of these take only three or four days in the pyramid, as long as I put in only a small handful. The extraordinary thing about mummified herbs and condiments is that they taste positively fresh and retain their true colour when compared to commercially dried or dehydrated ones, which keep some flavour but definitely lose their original vital colour. I have some celery and mint leaves that are four years old and still look and smell as fresh as the day I bought them. Unfortunately for my

---

* These specimens may be placed on the floor or base of the pyramid.

four-year-old rose, I put some of the celery leaves in the same box with the rose, and the celery scent was so strong that now my lovely yellow rose smells just like celery.

Two of my friends have made raisins from white seedless grapes. They report that it takes 6 to 8 weeks, depending on the size of the grapes and how many you put in the pyramid at one time. It is best to put in only a dozen or so. The delightful thing about mummified raisins is that they do not taste like raisins but rather like fresh grapes, no matter how old they get.

Another thing I have done with a pyramid is to pull a string up through the point at the top and hang the pyramid about 12 inches up over an ailing plant. In just a few days the plant perked up, and by the end of a week, it was thriving.

Trying to make honey drops was my most curious experiment. I didn't get honey drops, but I did get some intriguing results. I poured two tablespoons of honey in a very small shallow dish and centred it on the box top in the pyramid. Five days later, the honey had become sticky and tacky. A week after this, it had begun to solidify. And after 3 weeks, I could tip the dish up on its side for almost a minute before the honey began to slide to one side. Then someone accidentally moved the pyramix from the true geographic north-south axis, and when I checked it at the end of the fourth week, to my amazement the honey had turned to liquid.

I realigned the pyramid and waited, and it resolidified to the same degree after 3 weeks. Just for fun, I unaligned the pyramid to see if the honey would melt a second time. It did, and then resolidified after being realigned. This time I left the honey in the pyramid 6 weeks before looking at it, and then took it out and turned the dish on end. The honey seemed quite firm and only slipped a little in the very centre, sort of like a small bulge. So I put it back for another week and finally it was done. No matter how hard I pressed my finger into the honey, it did not stick, and my finger made only a very slight depression in the honey. It had a smooth, rubbery consistency. I kept the honey for several months on display on my end table, and then when it had collected quite a bit of dust on it, I wiped it off with a damp cloth without damaging the honey. The next time the honey got dusty, I decided to wash it off under running water, and you guessed it. The honey melted.

After someone told me about an article in *Time* magazine in which Gloria Swanson revealed that she slept with a pyramid under her bed because it gave her more energy. I promptly placed a red one under my bed more or less positioned so that it would be under my solar plexus. I was so full of energy the next day that I felt as though I had had a full 8 hours of sleep instead of only 5. I tried other colour pyramids under me, but for me (and it may be different for others), I seemed to get the most energy from the red, orange, purple, and pink in descending order. But all of them made me feel more energized in the morning. After I reported this to a friend of mine, the same night she put one under her bed so that it would be directly under her head, with the hope that in the morning her mind would be sharp and clear instead of her usual foggy state when she first got up. The next day she called to say it worked and that there was an immense difference. Soon she was waking up every day with her mind sharp and clear.

I thought about this, and then hypothesized that since there was so much energy coming out of the pyramid and being absorbed by my body while I slept, if I placed two more pyramids under the bed – one under each hip, thus forming a pyramid shape in itself with the one under my solar plexus – perhaps this pyramid-shaped energy would possibly melt off some of my excess fat. I did this for several weeks. My energy level was extraordinary, but neither my scale nor my tape measure would confirm any decrease in the size of my hips. However, I still put a pyramid under my solar plexus while I sleep whenever I feel the need for more energy. And most of my friends do, too.

Occasionally, for whatever reasons, I get a pain in my right hip. One day the pain was quite intense, so I decided to see if placing a pyramid under my chair would lessen my discomfort. Actually, I was sitting on a bench – one of those camel saddles – and with a little manoeuvering I was able to get the pyramid directly under my right hip. After a half-hour or so, the pain seemed to be a little less intense. Then I got up to answer the phone and came back to my seat and resumed my work. In about an hour, I noticed some strange feelings which I tried to ignore. After all, it was only 3 o'clock in the afternoon, and these feelings didn't usually occur till evening, and then not at all if I were alone. Thirty minutes later, it was becoming more difficult to ignore the pleasant tingling sensations that were spreading here, there, and everywhere throughout my body. I walked across the room and dialed my boyfriend's number to see if he would like to come over a little earlier – right now would not be too soon. He was delighted and quite amused at my predicament and very happy to oblige. When I turned away from the phone, I noticed that the bench was now directly over the pyramid instead of to one side, and for an instant I wondered if the position of the pyramid had anything to do with my delightful tingly feelings.

Several weeks later, my boyfriend was going through a phase of being too tired to do anything but sit and watch TV. I gave him a pyramid to put under his bed, but he thought it was silly. A few days later, I got a brainstorm and put a red pyramid under his chair. Although he said that he was tired when he first arrived, after an hour or so after dinner, he announced that he felt revived and as a matter of fact 'full of energy'. I smiled innocently. I should like to report that red pyramids under tired boyfriends work miracles, and everyone should have at least one pyramid on hand just in case. (Note: he still doesn't know what I did, but will find out when he reads this book.)

This experiment did not end here, although what happened next was totally unplanned. Actually, I never bothered to remove the pyramid from under the chair, and my cleaning lady, who was used to finding pyramids under the bed, just left it there. And then one day in September a member of the International Association for Psychotronic Research dropped by to discuss some of the papers that had been given at the First International Congress of Parapsychology and Psychotronic Research that had been held in Prague, Czechoslovakia, in June 1973, for which I had served as Western Hemisphere coordinator.

We had tea and had talked for at least two hours when I noticed that the gentleman seemed to be uncomfortable. He was sort of moving around in the chair and adjusting and readjusting his position, and his cheeks were flushed. His discomfort seemed to be increasing, so I studied him carefully and tuned in to him psychically to see what was bothering him: his body was definitely tingling and excited. At that moment I realized that the little red pyramid was still under that chair, and I smiled from ear to ear as I suggested that he might be more comfortable in another chair. He, too, is quite psychic and had perceived that something out of the ordinary was taking place. He moved his seat and after another hour, he spoke openly, stating that when he was sitting in the other chair, he had felt a curious energy rising up throughout his body which quite frankly had aroused him sexually but which, he said apologetically, he felt had nothing to do with my presence. He asked me if there was by any chance anything under the chair to account for his reaction. I laughed gleefully and recounted what I call the 'pyramid tingling effect' story or sometimes the 'cure for a tired boyfriend syndrome'. He was delighted and amused with the explanation, purchased some pyramids, and promised to share the results of his experiments.

I left the pyramid under that chair for almost a year, and I wish to report that all but three of the dozens and dozens of people (ladies, too) who have sat there have had similar experiences. Only one became angry. Most of them buy a pyramid and rush home to try it out on their own relatives and friends. Then in a few weeks, they call to share their experiences. Try it and see if you agree.

Max Toth loaned me a 6-foot pyramid that had plastic sides that reached almost to the floor. The frame was made of wooden dowels. Often when I felt my mind was a little sluggish, I moved my work, the phone, a pillow, and me into the pyramid. I am petite, so I can stretch out full length lying on my tummy and edit or proofread quite comfortably while soaking up energy. In about 15 minutes I usually notice that the cobwebs are gone from my brain and that my pencil is flying over the pages. I catch more errors, and the rate of editing or proofing accelerates. I have stayed working in there for as long as 2 hours. Then I seem to be completely revitalized and go back to working at my desk.

Sometimes, for fun I have tried working with a little pyramid on my head like a hat, but it isn't nearly as effective as working inside the big pyramid. An additional side benefit of working in the pyramid is that when I have had a slight headache or any other ache or pain, including cramps, it will disappear within an hour.

In my weekly workshop for developing psychic abilities that I conducted during this time, we did many experiments with telepathy in the big pyramid. Just sitting in it, many of these people reported seeing flashes of colour, having prickly sensations on their skin, hearing music, and increased sense perception. Some of them receive and send telepathic messages more accurately than they do outside the pyramid. One fascinating experiment was sending out colours to the person sitting in the pyramid. Almost everyone in our group of 12 has an accuracy of 8 or 9 hits out of 10 tries in receiving colours which I have sent them telepathically. However, when receiving inside the pyramid, this group consistently reported seeing white when I sent red, and then red when I had sent white. Or they interchanged black and white. Green is often received as a flash of yellow and immediately a flash of blue or vice versa. Some colours are received exactly as sent. I will not give all the various interchanges here, because you may wish to try this experiment yourself, and knowing all the variations would spoil it for you.

The group as a whole did very well with telepathically receiving fruits and vegetables with the same accuracy inside the pyramid as they did outside it. Some of the members of this group use their big pyramids for meditation. They report that if they stay in too long (time varies from person to person), they feel light-headed or slightly dizzy, as opposed to their feelings of euphoria or of being a little 'high' after shorter periods in the pyramid. We have speculated that this might occur with taller people whose heads reach up into the upper third of the pyramid where there is less oxygen and so the person would sometimes be rebreathing his own carbon dioxide. A simple solution to this is to leave more space between the lower edges of the pyramid sides and the floor or every once in a while raise one of the sides of the pyramid to allow fresh air in. Another favourable report of benefit from sitting in the large pyramid is that people with colds seem to be able to clear out their heads in just an hour or two and have lasting relief from the cold symptoms long after they come out of the pyramid.

Currently, I teach a weekly workshop called 'Beyond Alpha: How to Develop Psychic Abilities' to a group of Silva Mind Control graduates. When I was showing them how to do telekinesis (moving objects without touching them), one of the students got the idea of putting his pyramid on the floor between his feet to increase his energy and help him move the objects (metal cigar tubes, batteries, ping-pong balls). It really worked, and in less time than usual, he became very proficient at moving even large size flashlight batteries. From this I got the idea to hold the cigar tubes over the pyramid to increase the energy. But to my surprise and disappointment, it neutralized them so that no one could get them to move for several minutes until we re-energized them with our own psychic energy. Then I tried placing the cigar tubes inside the pyramid for 10 minutes. And again they became neutralized completely. Then I held my hands over two pyramids for about 5 minutes; for the next 15 minutes I could not move any of the objects, not even the ping-pong ball.

The question my students ask most often about pyramid energy is which colour gives the most energy. There is no definitive answer to this question, for it varies from person to person. I prefer red, orange, pink, purple, in that order, and although there are many people who would agree with me, there are an equal number who prefer yellow, blue, green, black in that order. One way of deciding, of course, is to try out the different colours and see if you perceive a difference in energy output. Another way is to do the pendulum test by suspending a pendulum over the pyramid about 3 to 6 inches above the peak. Then observe which way the pendulum swings, counterclockwise (negative energy) or clockwise (positive energy) and which direction gives a more forceful swing. I think you will find that it concurs more with your personal colour preference than with any scientific cause.

My next experiment will be placing alfalfa seeds and mung beans in a pyramid for three days before sprouting them. Someone has suggested to me that this will yield a more bountiful crop of sprouts and that it will cut down on the sprouting time. What will your next experiment be? Whatever it is, I wish you success and joy. Enjoy.

13

Pyramids: Voyage into the Future

Imagine a gleaming white pyramid 853 feet high, with a spire of 212 feet and slope angle of 5 degrees, set in the financial district of one of the largest cities in the United States.

> The Pyramid's tapered shape makes each floor a different size. Thus tenants requiring as little as 2000 square feet can occupy an entire floor. The largest floor, the 5th, measures 149 feet per side, and contains about 22,000 square feet of space. The smallest, the 48th, measures only 45 feet per side. Elevators in the Pyramid are arranged to match building traffic needs and provide minimum interruption of views from perimeter offices. Of 18 high-speed elevators, four serve the narrow floors above the 27th floor 'sky lobby' and only two reach the top.

Is the above a quote from a new science fiction novel? No. It is the advertising copy put out by the real estate company selling space in 'The Transamerica Pyramid'. Billed as 'A San Francisco Landmark Since 1972', this building is the first in the United States to be constructed in the pyramid shape (see Figure 35).

However, the Transamerica Pyramid was not unique for too long. In 1974, the Unity Church of Christianity in Houston, Texas, erected a pyramid church in scale proportion to the Great Pyramid of Giza. This idea was conceived by the church's minister, John D. Rankin, and captured the interest of the entire construction industry. The building covers a total area of 9206 square feet and is a total of $63\frac{1}{2}$ feet high. In order to assure that the pyramid was oriented on the true north axis, a staff member of Houston's Burde Baker Planetarium was called in as a consultant, and it is now alleged that the church is aligned sixty times more accurately with true north than is the Great Pyramid itself.

The sides of the church, like those of the Great Pyramid, are the same length as the base, minus 5 per cent. The 89-foot square base is eight feet above the ground, allowing the space underneath to be used for maintenance rooms, restrooms, etc. The total pyramid effect is accomplished by surrounding the entire structure with sloping grass berms. A wide expanse of glass has been used for the main entry and the entire pyramid is covered with gold coloured aluminium siding.

In the interior, the sloping floor of the nave of the church allows for maximum visibility. The sanctuary seats 550 to 600 persons in the kind of seats used in theatres. Other interesting features include a slightly elevated altar and pulpit with rheostat controls for the lighting of the church, sound control systems in the chancel area, an upper choir loft and space for the organist.

The interior colours of the pyramid-church can be described as warm rather than bright. There is a predominance of natural wood and exposed brick walls.

Whether or not the users of these buildings will benefit from the pyramidal shapes remains to be seen. Certainly, it would be interesting to survey some of the job holders who work in the Transamerica Pyramid to find out if the shape of the building has affected them in any way – specifically, if they have noticed a decrease in tension and anxiety and/or an increase in their energy levels since they began spending eight hours a day, five days a week, inside the pyramid-shaped structure. Equally interesting would be to poll the parishioners of the Houston United Church of Christianity and discover whether or not they are experiencing a new-found sense of peace and fulfillment in the church and/or whether or not they believe their prayers are answered more often when they are offered inside a pyramid-shaped edifice.

Following the lead set by Transamerica and the Unity Church, Cheops, Inc., a California-based firm, is selling architectural plans to those individuals who wish to build their own pyramid-houses. Although they have been selling these plans for several years, we have not as yet been able to obtain any information as to how well the business is doing, or how the owner/builders are reacting to living in pyramid-houses.

We believe that these pyramid buildings are just the beginning – the progenitors of an entire civilization of pyramid structures used for an infinite variety of purposes.

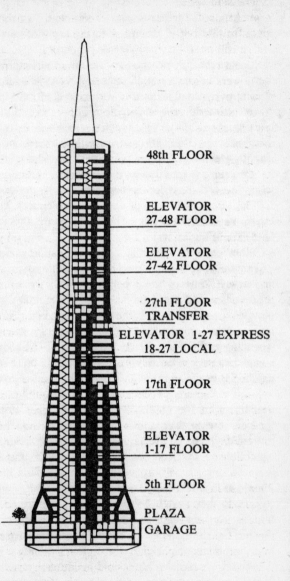

48th FLOOR

ELEVATOR
27-48 FLOOR

ELEVATOR
27-42 FLOOR

27th FLOOR
TRANSFER

ELEVATOR 1-27 EXPRESS
18-27 LOCAL

17th FLOOR

ELEVATOR
1-17 FLOOR

5th FLOOR

PLAZA
GARAGE

Figure 35. The Transamerica Pyramid. A San Francisco Landmark Since 1972.

Pyramids in Space

It would also be interesting to experiment with the pyramid in outer space, to find out if, when not in the sway of earth's magnetic force field, it still retains its inexplicable properties.

Should research prove that even in an extraterrestrial atmosphere, the powers of the pyramid still exist, NASA might want to consider placing pyramidal structures in spacecraft to aid in the prolonging of flights into outer space. At present there is some research going on into the use of the freezing process as a means of slowing down the metabolic rate of an astronaut so that a few years could physiologically have no more effect on a human than a few minutes. Perhaps the pyramid, with its preservative powers, could be used as a supplemental aid, or even a substitute, for this cryogennic process.

Pyramids as Power Sources

It is natural to wonder if there is not some way in which the pyramid could be used to light and supply needed electrical power to small cities. One suggestion is that perhaps solar energy could be absorbed and stored in a pyramid constructed of the most viable materials possible for absorbing the electromagnetic energy of the sun. Or perhaps some form of generator could be operated on the tremendous heat energy contained in a giant pyramid. Still another possibility is that scientists will discover that a pyramid constructed of some type of metal, or oriented on the north-south axis, will become magnetically charged to the extent that it could provide power to light homes.

Some researchers have suggested that the pyramid shape might be used for focusing the highly structured laser beam. Perhaps lasers focused through the apices of pyramids could be used to disperse threatening storms in instances where loss of life and property damage is possible.

Pyramids in Education and Health Care

Pyramids might also be particularly well-suited for use as study booths in schools and institutions of higher education. If, as claimed, the pyramid is capable of both relaxing and energizing individuals, many students might find their mental acuity vastly improved by doing their research or homework inside such structures.

If, as mystics claim, the pyramid tent does induce an altered state of consciousness, people learning to control their own brain waves through the application of biofeedback techniques might be aided considerably if their training were to be conducted inside these tents.

Ostrander and Schroeder quote Karl Drbal as saying, 'Some researchers believe if hospitals were built in (the pyramid) form, patients would get better faster ...' Other medical personnel are beginning to wonder if pyramid tents might not be used as an aid to the natural healing process. Pyramidologists suggest that certain spots inside the pyramid have a 'vibration level' corresponding to certain physiological organs. Consequently, sitting in one spot in the pyramid tent might be of great benefit to a heart patient, whereas sitting in an entirely different position might facilitate the healing process of a person recovering from a kidney infection. Some people have even gone so far as to speculate that childbirth might be facilitated inside a pyramid.

Pyramid containers have been suggested for storage of drugs. Such storage could add months, or even years to the shelf-life of the pharmaceuticals.

Considering that the relaxing effects of the pyramid have been so highly touted, it is not surprising that some people are claiming that pyramid-therapy will be the newest form of psycho-therapy.

Other Applications of Pyramid Power

On a more prosaic level, pyramids might be used inside our homes as cupboards or canisters which would help to preserve grains, dried fruits, nuts and perhaps even produce.

It is even possible that the day will come when entire supermarkets will be constructed in the pyramid shape. Or perhaps the cereal and dry food sections might be built in pyramid form. Carrying this suggestion one step further, perhaps grain storage elevators could be constructed in pyramid form. If these could preserve grains longer than the present structures can, they would certainly be useful in a world in which the population is expanding and food shortage could become a serious problem.

As we have already mentioned, many people have discovered the relaxing effects of the pyramid-tents. But one tent user has come up with a new twist. This California businessman claims that the tent not only gives him a spiritual lift, but improves his sexual desires. This does not come as a surprise to some occultists, who claim that certain parts of the pyramid correspond to parts of the human body; carrying this one step further, they claim that specific parts of the anatomy correlate to certain chambers in the Great Pyramid. Thus, the unfinished chamber, often called the grotto, corresponds to the sexual organs, the King's Chamber corresponds to the mind and the Queen's Chamber to the heart.

It will be interesting to follow, throughout the next few years, the progress made by amateur and professional researchers in the new field of pyramidology. We look forward to seeing the uses of the miniature pyramid expand, and to learning of the construction of new pyramid-shaped buildings.

Ancient Advanced Technology

The great pyramids of the world are masterpieces of architecture, engineering and construction. In fact, these colossal monuments cannot be replicated, let alone duplicated, by our modern technology. It therefore seems incredible that members of ancient civilizations, using no mechanical or electrical equipment, were able to create these unique structures. Yet this is precisely what we are asked to believe by archaeologists and historians who, because they have found only crude implements, on the sites where these structures were built, refuse to accept even the possibility that other, more highly advanced tools might have been used.

It seems to us that to refuse to accept anything but the evidence of our eyes in so paradoxical a situation is to close our minds — and possibly preclude our ever finding a solution to a mystery that has plagued and intrigued humankind for centuries.

We believe that there is a strong possibility that at one time a race inhabited the earth which had a technology so advanced that it is impossible for us to imagine it. We derive this belief from these several facts:

1. Pyramids have been built on different sites all around the world which are virtually identical in terms of architecture, engineering, masonry and astronomical orientation.

2. None of these pyramids could have been built with the implements found at their sites.

3. On the Plain of Nazca in Peru, a country noted for its pyramids, are a series of markings which, according to Erich Von Däniken in *Chariots of the Gods?*, are 'very reminiscent of the aircraft parking areas in a modern airport'.

4. A large number of drawings and sculptures have been unearthed at excavation sites in the same general areas as the pyramids, which depict people clothed and helmeted in a fashion very similar to

modern flyers and astronauts.

5. Statues have been uncovered in South America depicting a variety of racial types, most of whom should have been unknown to the people who ostensibly created these figures.

6. Mummification was practiced by all of the pyramid-building peoples.

7. In ancient Peru, skulls have been uncovered which show positive evidence of extraordinarily skilful and successful brain surgery. Also found at the sites were over twenty implements used by the ancient surgeons. According to a highly respectable Peruvian neuro-surgeon, more than 85 per cent of the operations performed were successful. By today's standards this is a phenomenal percentage.

8. As far as can be ascertained, the religious practices of all the pyramidal civilizations show a remarkable number of similarities.

All of these facts indicate to us that there were, in what is known as prehistoric time, people capable not only of constructing inimitable edifices and of making the most precise astronomical calculations, but also of executing highly complex surgical techniques, of travelling around an astensibly unnavigable world, and of creating the impression, through the use of a highly developed technology, that they were gods.

The Nature of the Gods

In both the Old and New Testaments, there are references to 'gods' and implications that those who received the words of God as originally spoken, and later written down in the Bible, were also gods.

I have said, ye are gods; and all of you are children of the most High.

Psalms, 82;6.

Jesus answered: 'It is written in your own law that God said, "You are gods". We know that what the scripture says is true for ever; and God called them gods, those people to whom his message was given.'

John, 10;35 (as quoted in
Good News for Modern Man)

Jesus, who called himself 'the son of God', has been imbued by his worshippers with godlike qualities. Similarly, other great spiritual leaders, such as Buddha and Mohammed, were considered to be gods by their followers. It is interesting to note that the disciples of each of these men built a religion based around him to the point where the name of the man and the theology were merged, e.g. Christianity; Buddhism. Equally interesting is the fact that these men, or 'gods', lived rather similar lives and preached the same basic doctrines. It was only as the religions grew that the worshippers began to obscure the basic techniques and teachings with rites, rituals, philosophies and traditions of their own, so that today, religions founded on virtually the same ethics have such vastly different outward trappings that their similarities are extremely difficult to discern.

In *Pagan and Christian Creeds*, Edward Carpenter lists ten basic characteristics which all of the gods who walked the earth had in common:

1. They were born on or very near the 25th of December.
2. They were born of a virgin mother.
3. They led a life of toil for humankind.
4. They were born in a nave or underground chamber.
5. They were called by such names as 'The Lightbringer', 'Healer', 'Meditator', 'Saviour', 'Deliverer'.
6. They were vanquished by the so-called powers of darkness.
7. They descended into an underworld.
8. They rose again from the dead, and became the champions of humankind in the heavenly world.
9. Communions of saints were founded around them and churches were begun into which disciples were received by baptism.
10. They were commemorated by eucharistic meals.

One example of a deity who, like Christ, incorporated the above-described characteristics was the Egyptian god Osiris.

According to Plutarch, Osiris was born on the 361st day of the year. Like Christ, he travelled a great deal. He became King of Egypt and 'tamed (his subjects) by music and gentleness, not by force of arms'. Plutarch recounts that he was betrayed by the powers of darkness, slain and dismembered. 'This happened,' he says, 'on the 17th of the month of Athyr, when the sun goes into the Scorpion.' His body was placed in a coffin from which, two days later, he rose. Every year thereafter, in commemoration of his resurrection, an image in a coffin was brought out before the worshippers who would greet it, crying, 'Osiris is Risen'.

The Creator god, worshipped by the Peruvians, was also described as one who travelled widely across his country, teaching the people.

Unlike most of the others, Viracocha was not killed and resurrected. Instead, he simply left the continent, by walking across the Pacific Ocean.

So great are the similarities between the lives – and deaths – of the so-called gods, or great spiritual leaders, that it is impossible to resist the suggestion that the appearance, time and time again, in different parts of the world, of such nearly identical figures was far from coincidental. Indeed, it seems as if each of these men had been chosen, perhaps as a saviour, more likely as an initiate, to get out among the people and undergo virtually identical experiences.

When it is recalled that every one of these figures lived within close proximity of a pyramid complex, Manly P. Hall's description in *The Secret Teachings of All Ages* of the ritual enacted in the Great Pyramid takes on fresh significance:

> In the King's Chamber was enacted the drama of 'the second death'. Here the candidate, after being crucified upon the cross of the solstices and the equinoxes, was buried in the great coffer ...

> The candidate was laid in the great stone coffin, and for three days his spirit – freed from its mortal coil – wandered at the gateways of eternity ... Realizing that his body was a house which he could slip out of and return to without death, he achieved actual immortality. At the end of three days he returned to himself again, and having thus personally ... experienced the great mystery, he was indeed an initiate – one who beheld and one to whom religion had fulfilled her duty bringing him to the light of God.

Hall also writes:

> The King's Chamber was ... a doorway between the material world and the transcendental spheres of Nature ... Thus in one sense the Great Pyramid may be likened to a gate through which the ancient priests permitted a few to pass toward the attainment of individual completion.

It has been suggested by one theorist that the 'few' who were permitted to pass were the survivors of the Atlantean Civilization, sent out by the priests to bring enlightenment to the people of the particular region in which, or near to which, there was a pyramid. In each instance, the 'initiate' would travel the country, teaching, comforting and healing the people and then, in a mysterious fashion, vanish. In every case, however, twelve disciples, or apostles, would be left behind to insure that the memory of the teacher, now called a god, or saviour, by the people, would be kept alive, and his teachings preserved for posterity.

A tantalizing suggestion, but one which leaves a number of questions unanswered. For instance:

Why was the ritual always so precisely the same – why did the initiate have to be born at the same time, die in the same manner, etc.?

Were there a number of Atlantean colonies around the world – perhaps one at each pyramidal site? Or was there just one, which had mastered the science of air travel and which flew around the world, from pyramid centre to pyramid centre, picking up new initiates and bringing knowledge to the people of the earth as it travelled?

What happened to the members of this highly technologized society? Did they die out? Were they killed in some natural disaster? Or might they still be alive in some still unknown and inaccessible part of the world?

There is another interesting fact which might lend credence to the contention that the builders of the pyramids were, in fact, members of an advanced race with the ability to pilot aircraft. It has been noted that most of the peoples of the so-called prehistoric civilizations were fire worshippers. The only exceptions were the peoples of pyramidal civilizations – all of whom were sun worshippers. When combined with the fact that these people have left behind them a collection of sculptures and drawings depicting helmeted figures bearing an astounding resemblance to modern airmen, the conclusion is almost inescapable that the 'sun gods', to whom these various civilizations paid homage, were actually flyers from some earthly master race.

Writes Von Däniken in *Chariots of the Gods?*, 'The Spanish conquistadors who conquered South and Central America came up against the sagas of Viracocha (the Peruvian god) everywhere. Never before had they heard of gigantic white men who came from somewhere in the sky ... They learned about a race of *sons of the sun* (authors' emphasis added) who instructed mankind in all kinds of arts and disappeared again. And in all the legends ... there was an assurance that the sons of the sun would return.'

If, in fact, these 'sons of the sun' were members of a master race who piloted aircraft from one civilization to another, it is possible that they deliberately built their temples and initiation centres in the shape of pyramids so that the vortices of energy, rising from the apices of the structures, would serve as beacons to returning pilots. And the truncated, or flat-topped, or terraced pyramids, which inevitably crop up in every pyramidal civilization, could have been constructed to do double duty as temples and also as landing pads for aircraft.

As we pointed out earlier in this chapter, there is substantial evidence that highly advanced techniques were practised upon members of ancient civilizations. The practitioners of these techniques were also expert in the art of mummification. In fact, this science was known to members of every pyramidal civilization.

In *Chariots of the Gods?* Erich Von Däniken points out that the corpses found in Egyptian tombs were apparently embalmed for a corporeal return, since they were buried with a substantial variety of material goods, including money and jewelry. 'Drawings and sagas actually indicated that the "gods" promised to return from the stars in order to awaken the well-preserved bodies to new life.'

Von Däniken goes on to speculate that possibly 'the pharaoh, who certainly knew more about the nature and customs of the "gods" than his subjects had (reasoned) ... "I must make a burial place for myself that cannot be destroyed for millennia and is visible far across the country. The gods promised to return and wake me up (or doctors in the distant future will discover a way to restore me to life again)." '

At first sight, this seems to be a most reasonable theory, particularly in light of the apparent preservative powers of the pyramid, which might very well have aided in preserving the mummy until medical practitioners arrived to restore the body to life. There is however, a serious flaw to this hypothesis: If the mummies were embalmed for the specific purpose of corporeal return, why were the brains and viscera inevitably removed? Is Von Däniken completely wrong in his interpretation of the reason for the elaborate embalming procedures? Or did the embalmers anticipate total organ transplants when their 'gods' returned?

One peculiarity to pyramidal structures throughout the world is their lack of capstones. Rarely has a pyramid been discovered with the capstone (if it ever existed) still intact. We are frankly at a loss to explain this oddity, nor could we find any other researchers who could explain it from an architectural or scientific point of view. The only author who offers any explanation at all is Hall, who writes, in *The Secret Teachings of All Ages:*

The size of the capstone of the Great Pyramid cannot be accurately determined, for, while most investigators have assumed that it was once in place, no vestige of it now remains. There is a curious tendency among the builders of great religious edifices to leave their creations unfinished, thereby signifying that God is alone complete. The capstone – if it existed – was itself a miniature pyramid, the apex of which again would be capped by a smaller block of similar shape, and so on *ad infinitum*. The capstone therefore is the epitome of the entire structure. Thus, the Pyramid may be likened to the universe and the capstone to man. Following the chain of analogy, the mind is the capstone of man, the spirit the capstone of the mind, and God – the epitome of the whole – the capstone of the spirit. As a rough and unfinished block, man is taken from the quarry and by the secret culture of the Mysteries gradually transformed into a trued and perfect pyramidal capstone. The temple is complete only when the initiate himself becomes the living apex through which the divine power is focused into the diverging structure below.

For thousands of years, pyramids have captivated the imaginations of scholars, historians, architects, archaeologists, and mystics. These great monuments still stand, on remote sites in inaccessible regions of the earth. Massive and mute, they are the guardians of a wisdom greater than our present civilization has ever known – or might ever know.

Possibly, current experiments with pyramids will provide us the key to discovering the mystery of the pyramids of the past. Or, they may simply enable us to utilize the pyramid's shape to solve many of the environmental and technological problems of the future.

14

The Future is Now!

In the preparation of this second revised and enlarged edition of Pyramid Power, *many new applications, experiments, and discoveries have come to our attention. We have written this chapter in order to share a few of these growing possibilities and investigate with you some of the new utilization of pyramid energies and shapes.*

A great deal of practical interest is being focused on the meditation pyramid – those larger models in which you stand, sit, sleep, or make love. A meditation pyramid should have several holes on each face a few inches from the apex for ventilation. In addition, the base should be raised an inch or two from the floor for proper air circulation while the pyramid is in use. Whether the pyramid has a solid wall or is plastic-covered, this precaution must be taken or you may suffer from anoxia, which is insufficient oxygen consumption leading to light-headedness, shortness of breath, and fainting. Although no reports of a fatal or even serious nature are known from the use of the meditation pyramid, negative feelings, headaches, and even euphoria during lovemaking may be the effect of what we term 'Meditation Pyramid Anoxia'. Until more data is available, we suggest you keep in mind that the length of time spent in a meditation pyramid is inversely proportional to the amount of oxygen-consuming activity. That is, the greater the activity, the less time should be spent inside. Sleeping consumes the least amount of oxygen, therefore the longer one can remain within.

Effects of Plastic Pyramids

The plastic-covered meditation pyramids or pyramid tents may pose additional influence on the occupants which could contaminate and perhaps even negate the effects sought for. It is well known that plastic materials build up or accumulate static electricity more easily and readily on their surfaces than do most other substances. The friction involved while setting up the pyramid can cause hundreds and even thousands of volts to accumulate on the plastic surfaces. This static electricity is similar to the type which your body acquires while walking across a rug during a cool, dry day. Touching a light switch will discharge this static voltage build-up through a sharp spark – and we all know how annoying that can be! Static electrical build-up on the plastic-covered pyramid rarely will result in giving you a shock. Rather, what will occur is a change in the electrical property of the air within the pyramid itself. This change in which the molecules of air either gain or lose electrons is called ionization. The process is enhanced as your body heat warms the air inside the pyramid, causing air currents which lead to stratifications of heat. The developing layers of temperature, warmer air at the top and cooler air at the bottom, will also ionize to various degrees of either positivity or negativity, depending on the static charge of the plastic covering. N.A.S.A. scientists have determined that people exposed to an environment with an atmosphere charged with negative ions are more alert and in general feel very good, while the opposite effect is experienced in a positively ionized atmosphere. Here the person experiences different levels of depression or simply a negative feeling. This fact strongly suggests that ionization of the air inside a plastic-covered meditation pyramid could severely mask or alter the actual energies of the pyramid.

This ionization effect may very well be the cause for the reports of varying success in the use of plastic pyramids for plant growth enhancement. Generally, placing an ailing plant or one whose growth rate you wish speeded up into a plastic transparent or translucent pyramid will show remarkable changes within a week to ten days. However, occasionally there will be no change, while in other instances the plant will actually wither and die.

Basically, the many reports we have received from people all over the world contending that there are evil or negative aspects to the energies of the pyramid have arrived at this conclusion through faulty assumptions. Energies in their simplest and purest form, especially those in the pyramid shape, have neither a good nor an evil motivating factor. Energy is simply just that – energy. Energy can only affect change in that to which it is applied. Good and evil is the human rationalization for the relative change brought about by energy. In all properly documented cases presented to us alledgedly involving evil or negative forces of the pyramid, these results have definitely been an effect of either 'Meditation Pyramid Anoxia' or ionization effects. In many cases the two effects can not be separated, and therefore the results are the combination of both.

No effect or the seemingly opposite effect from the one which you had expected is definitely not a result of the power of the pyramid; rather it is the influence of many variables which actually cancel or block the energies of pyramid power. If this should happen with your use of the pyramid, we suggest you repeat your experiment in a different room at an interval of several days, or even weeks, later.

Pyramid Water

Water treated in the pyramid has become a useful product of pyramid power in the past few years. Not only is it free and plentiful, but water is the most practical substance to work with and virtually affects every moment of our lives. It is well known by aquarists that ordinary tap water should be allowed to 'age' three to four days before placing it into a fish tank. This ageing process allows fluorine, chlorine, and other chemicals to dissipate from the water. Other water-processing procedures consisting of boiling, filtering, and distilling, remove bacteria, minerals, and other contaminants. But this process is time-consuming and expensive, which is why bottled spring water is popular these days. Grandmother and great-grandmother circumvented this problem by using rain water to wash their hair and for other household purposes. Rain water is very soft, mineral-free, and relatively pure in content.

Now, regardless of the type of water you prefer, treating it in a pyramid imparts to it tremendous energetic properties with unlimited potential uses. The amount of water treatable depends on the size of the pyramid. We suggest that you treat a minimum of a quart of water at a time. The size of the pyramid should be large enough to allow the mid-point of the water container to be at the one-third level of the pyramid. We have found that a quart of water should be treated within the pyramid for at least 24 hours before use. Many people report that they have equivalent success with the water after only eight hours of treatment, but they usually use less than a quart.

After treating the water, cap the container and place it in the refrigerator or any other place which is fairly cool and relatively sunlight-free. Once water has been treated in the pyramid it can be stored for an indefinite period of time because its newly acquired energies are basically 'locked' to the water molecules. Once you have several quarts of pyramid water or even gallons accumulated, you can discover unlimited applications and uses and have a constant supply available. Water, by the way, is not the only liquid capable of absorbing the tremendous properties of pyramid energies. Use milk, any kind of beverage, even soup. After 24 hours, these liquids will taste much better than their untreated counterparts.

Pyramid water is being used for drinking purposes with reportedly beneficial and even curative results. People and pets drinking pyramid water alledgedly feel and look better. Your pet's coat will appear shinier and lusher. Songbirds fed pyramid water sing better, and the colourful plumage of birds in general will be brighter. We have received reports that soaking arthritic joints in pyramid water relieves, and in some instances eliminates, the pain and problems related to arthritis. Applying pyramid water to cuts, burns, bruises, moles, calluses, hangnails, warts, and various skin problems appears to be a definite adjunct to the normal medication used for treatment. Washing your hair with pyramid water and your favourite shampoo reportedly controls and even eliminates dandruff within four applications. Try using pyramid water to rinse tired eyes and even soak your contact lenses in it; the soothing effect is felt in seconds. Take your medicines and effervescent analgesic alkalizing powders or tablets with pyramid water rather than with plain tap water.

In the kitchen, pyramid water does wonders. Food cooked or even just soaked in pyramid water develops a better taste and quality. Coffee, tea, dried milk, orange juice, cocoa, pudding, condensed or dry soups, etc., appear to be greatly enhanced. Actually, pyramid water substituted for plain water for any use will be noticed immediately. Even the best cook will receive new praises. If your supply should happen to run short, pyramid water can be diluted as much as 2 parts plain water and 1 part pyramid water with very little effective loss of energies.

Pyramid water used for horiticultural purposes is a very effective adjunct or alternative if you do not wish to clutter your house with small pyramids to stimulate plant growth. Simply water your plants with pyramid water rather than plain tap water. Your plants and seedlings will definitely be enhanced in their growth rate, strength, and health. We are told that ailing, and in some cases dying, plants have recovered completely within 10 to 14 days. In your garden, pyramid water and tap water in equal parts will produce better flowers, fruits, vegetables, plants, bushes, and trees, and as a result you will have developed an even greener thumb. Of course, feeding your garden with hundred-percent pyramid water will benefit your weeds, as well, through the newfound energies, and this in turn will lead to additional work for you in the garden. Even so, the results will be well worth it. Here is a helpful hint: Place cut flowers in a vase filled with pyramid water and enjoy them for a much longer period of time – no need even to add a penny or aspirin tablet. Watering your lawn with hundred-percent nitrogen mixed with hundred-percent pyramid water will produce for you the greenest lawn in the neighbourhood. Your lawn will also be less susceptible to diseases and brown spotting.

Not surprisingly, those individuals who are completely turned off to pyramid power and who preach against it basically claim that the energies of the pyramid are totally devoid of scientific meaning. In essence, they are implying that the laws and foundations of science are now complete, and that no further addition or expansion to these laws is possible. 'If it doesn't fit into the existing realm of science, it doesn't exist.' We who have seriously studied pyramid power know that these energies do exist; we have seen the results. Even in science there are experiments which can not be successfully duplicated one hundred percent of the time but, when faithfully followed, will eventually unfold their mystery and receive admission into the 'laws of science'.

Those of you who wish to repeat a simple experiment within the 'laws of science' may do so using the research of Mr John Rex of New York City. In his experiment, Mr Rex recharged an ordinary battery placed in the pyramid. The following is the first publication of Mr Rex's experimental findings.

Experiment Purpose

To determine if a flashlight D-cell battery, which was at a low voltage, could be recharged to a higher voltage by being placed under a cardboard scale model of Cheops's Pyramid.

Controls

Three weak D-cell batteries of similar voltage were left outside of the pyramid as controls. In addition, a digital voltmeter was used to determine voltage to the fourth decimal place. That is 0.0001 volts or one ten-thousandths of a volt. A qualified technician measured all the voltages, both at the beginning and again at the end of the experiment.

Set-up of Experiment

Pyramid was aligned and situated as per instructions received with pyramid kit sold by the Toth Pyramid Company of New York City. Battery was placed at the 1/3 height within the pyramid with positive terminal pointing north and negative terminal pointing south.

Battery Voltages

Batteries not under pyramid – controls B, C and D

	Voltage at start	Voltage one month later	Net Change
[B]	1.312	1.3713	+0.0101 volts
[C]	1.3709	1.3742	+0.0033 volts
[D]	1.3593	1.3740	+0.0147 volts
[E] Average Change –			+0.0094 volts

Battery under pyramid

	Voltage at start	Voltage one month later	Net Change
[A]	1.3579	1.3776	+0.0197 volts

Results

Net change of battery under pyramid – [A]	0.0197
less largest net change of control battery [D]	0.0147
pyramid battery gained	0.0050 volts
Net change of battery under pyramid [A]	0.0197
less average net change of control batteries [E]	0.0094
pyramid battery gained	0.0103 volts

Comments and Conclusion

If we only compare the voltages of the control battery [D] which had the greatest net change of voltage against the pyramid battery [A], we find a gain of only 5 millivolts. Obviously, if we compare the pyramid battery [A] to the average change in the control batteries [E] voltage, we find we have an higher energy boost of 10.3 millivolts or twice as much. To go one step further, we could have compared the lowest control voltage [C] to the pyramid voltage [A] and produce a net change of 16.4 millivolts. In either case there is evidence of 'Pyramid Power'.

In his research report Mr Rex finds the pyramid to be a new source for recharging batteries and suggests that the pyramid shape can also influence mentality and stimulate psychic centres.

Pyramid Architecture

We have found that in the past five years the pyramid shape has definitely influenced our lives and even our vocabulary. More and more people are becoming pyramid conscious through the various media of books, magazines, newspapers, periodicals, television, radio and the like. The most practical application of pyramid power to gain recent popularity is the building of pyramid structures: restaurants, churches, office buildings, and homes.

Mr Robert Bruce Cousins, architect, has been gaining a steady growth of clientele for whom he is designing pyramid buildings. Mr Cousins claims that many of the architectural firms presently designing buildings in the shape of pyramids actually violate the esoteric and energy-producing powers of the pyramid. This, he says, is done by disturbing the continuity of the edges and grossly invading the faces of the pyramid shape. Mr Cousins constructed a pyramid in Malibu, California, as a demonstration of pyramid energy. It was constructed for future use as a residence and is now being used in such a way. The structure is very accurate and functions in powerful ways. Meditation experiences are sometimes astounding, and he was able to determine specific pathways of energy within the pyramid for future application. The energy generated in this thirty-foot-tall pyramid is extremely high. As an example, he was able to make an aurameter respond vigorously by concentrating a beam of energy through the palms of his hands and directed toward the aurameter at a distance of 22 feet.

There is a project planned by Mr Cousins for a vegetarian restaurant in Los Angeles for the New Age Atlanteans. A study of the plans shows public participation in pyramid energy — a pyramid within a pyramid — as well as the obvious benefits to a food establishment. He plans an extensive display of pyramid knowledge and the use of holography and laser lighting in the restaurant experience.

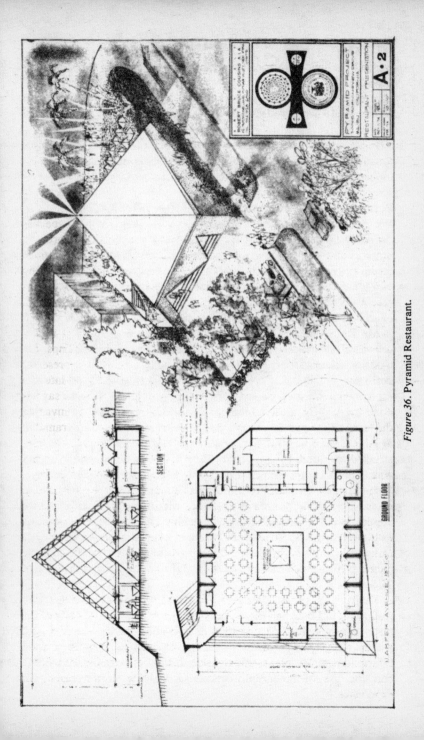

Figure 36. Pyramid Restaurant.

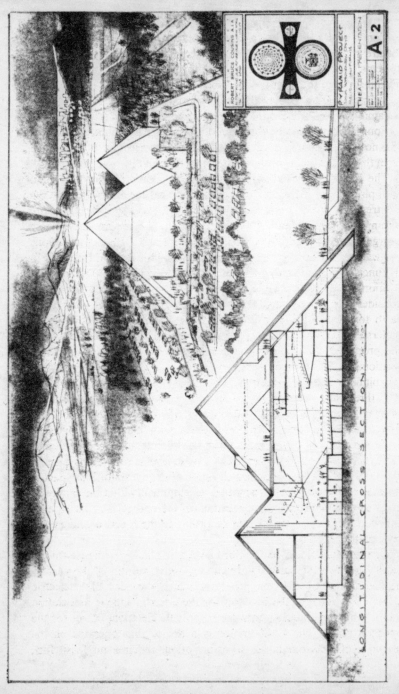

Figure 37. Pyramid Theatre.

Concurrently with the restaurant, plans for a 2500-seat pyramid theatre are projected for San Francisco. It utilizes advanced media systems and techniques. Imagine the theatrical experience being heightened by the energy developed by the immense pyramid. A restaurant seating 230 will be in Pyramidion location with its own pyramid for public use: a pyramid on a pyramid within a pyramid!

Four additional major constructions are in the planning stage which will not only become monumental works of perfection but also will form the classic basis for pyramid structure design.

The Centre for Spiritual Evolvement in California has the main level planned for activities that express the vital social involvement the Centre has with the community. Rising to the upper level, a pure pyramid space, bathed with coloured light, creates an atmosphere charged with an energy that uplifts the spirit and increases vibrations of awareness. The north-south orientation of the pyramid is basic to its function as a life energy accumulator and generator. The intrinsic relationship of the pyramid to the forces of nature is an important consideration in a pyramid design. The seasons and relationship of the earth to the sun establish the pyramid as a central benchmark for understanding man's relationship to the cosmos. The manner in which the proposed spiritual building is related to the site emphasizes the relationship between spiritual evolvement and the physical body we inhabit on the physical plane of awareness.

A three-storey residence in New York is planned to take advantage of energy forces developed within a pyramid as an accumulator. The first floor houses the basic living areas with kitchen, diningroom, bathrooms, and bedrooms. There is direct access to outdoor recreation spaces and gardens. The second level is reached by a spiral staircase and is at the one-third elevation of the pyramid. This space is devoted to the activities of spiritual development within the family. It is an area in which the concentration of life energy is at its highest. Individual use areas are located according to the function and energy level desired.

Directly above, and on the third level, is a glass greenhouse for the development of the basic family garden twelve months of the year. It also houses a wind-driven generator which provides basic electric needs and recharges the batteries for the electromagnetic association motor which operates a generator to provide electrical power for the pyramid home. The EMA motor is a device that operates on the principle of electromagnetic transformation, requires no fossil fuel,

Figure 38. Centre for Spiritual Evolvement.

recycles its own formation, requires no fossil fuel, recycles its own energy, and creates no waste. A self-contained organic treatment system that produces usable compost as an end product will dispose of solid waste products.

A pyramid complex is being designed for the Institute of Healing Sciences in New York. The Director and Founder, Mr Greg Finnegan, has set a programme to realize his philosophy through a series of spaces where individuals can come together to gain benefit from the many facets of Eastern and Western metaphysical sciences available today. The programme includes facilities for yoga, Transcendental Meditation, acupuncture, healing, positive mental attitude clinics, psycho-physical therapy clinics, psychic diagnostics, Western spiritual dynamics, the martial arts such as T'ai-Chi, and numerous other practices.

The architectural volumes of the Institute are resolved into five pyramids that contain spaces designed for specific uses. A lower level below grade and illuminated by skylights will house office, administration, storage, and mechanical spaces. A central meditation garden is located on the ground level under the great pyramid. Its seclusion will be assured by the four base pyramids shielding this area from external influences.

METAPARTMENTS – A New Age Multiple Dwelling – is suitable for any location. The pyramid contains secrets of cosmic wisdom and is therefore well suited for aware new age personalities to use as a residence. In this pyramid apartment structure one will not have to leave his home and travel to a separate centre for development. The community centre is a form created from a real and virtual pyramid suspended between two apartment pyra-walls providing ample space for small or large groups participating in metaphysical development activities. The apex pyramid at the highest point of the twelve-storey building houses a pure pyramid for use by the members of the pyramid community.

The METAPARTMENT structure is composed of precast-pre-tensioned concrete units which are prefabricated as building blocks. Each apartment will have through ventilation and be soundproof. A glass wall will span the length of the outside terrace overlooking the views which face east and west. The two triangular apartment walls provide cover for a private park and garden area on grade. This area will have a peaceful atmosphere, since all apartments face outward, in the direction opposite the recreation area, and thus sound is dispersed

Figure 39. Residence.

toward the outside and away from the interior park. Parking is underground and solar heat collectors are built into the fascia of each balcony as a natural source of energy.

Mr Cousins is currently working on a metaphysical centre, a garden centre, a therapy centre, and other residential designs for the pyramid as well as experimenting with other energy form generators and accumulators. The philosophy of applying metaphysical principles to architecture is termed by Mr Cousins 'METATECTURE'. It is the application of this philosophy which properly merges each geometric form and its own unique type of energy into a livable space. He also states that properly designing interior configurations, especially the pyramid form, is truly a time-consuming and thought-provoking experience, one in which a flamboyant attitude can not be used. His plans and drawings attest to the care he gives each project he undertakes.

Martian Pyramids

From architectural feats on earth we have recently been astounded to find pyramids on Mars! Four pyramidal-shaped structures, two small and two large, have appeared on some of the more than 7000 photographs beamed to earth during Mariner 9's flyby of Mars. Space scientists generally agree that these pyramidal shapes may not be of natural origin. The scientists claim to be able to approximately measure their size and height. However, they can not agree as to whether these structures are three- or four-faced. What are these structures, who built them, how many more are there, and where did they come from? These are questions to which the scientists are not able as yet to supply satisfactory answers. To us, evidence of extra-terrestial-type structures suggests the existence of civilizations differently evolved, though not necessarily more advanced than ours. This discovery alone raises questions far beyond the scope and purpose of this book; nevertheless, it certainly lends more credence to Von Däniken's and other related theories.

Another interesting phenomenon which scientific knowledge attempts to explain away is the existence of voice tape recordings. These tapes are made with ordinary tape recorders and microphones, or with the microphone input shorted out using a special plug. Thousands of tape recordings have been made for years now, producing raps, clicks, bells, whispers, chimes, muffled sound, breathing, as well as clearly audible words and phrases. Now the

Figure 40. Institute of Healing Sciences.

Figure 41. Metapartments.

pyramid has enabled the expansion of research for the paranormal tape researchers. In a recent book, *Talks with the Dead*, the author, William Welch, tells of placing a pyramid on his tape recorder while he recorded the spirit voices and found that the pyramid assisted in increasing the signals both in quality and quantity as recorded by the tape. This experiment suggests that there truly are unlimited uses and applications of the pyramidal form. More importantly, it impresses upon us that there exists the possibility of discovering new instrumentation capable of measuring, recording, and quantifying pyramid power.

The years to come will definitely bring us closer to a recovery of the extensive and intensive wisdom of the pyramids. To all of us who delve into this wisdom, the future holds out to us one of the most mysterious forces and greatest mysteries that the ancients have left as their legacy: **PYRAMID POWER.**

Bibliography

Adams, Walter Marsham. *The Book of The Master*. Putnam, New York, 1898; reprinted Aquarian Press, 1980.

Adler, *Mathematics for Science and Engineering*. McGraw-Hill.

Aldersmith, Herbert. *The Great Pyramid, Its Divine Message*. London, 1932.

Amkraut, Joel. 'Pyramid Power', *Spaceview Magazine*, Jan.-Feb., 1973.

Andrews, E. Wyllys. 'Chronology and Astronomy in the Maya Area' (in *The Maya and Their Neighbours*), pp. 150-161. New York, 1940.

Archibald, R.C. *Notes on Logarithmic Spiral of the Golden Section*. New Haven, 1920.

Archibald, R.C. *The Pyramids and Cosmic Energy*. Aleph Enterprises, Palo Alto, Cal., 1972.

Badaway, A. *A History of Egyptian Architecture*, Vols. I-III. Cairo, Berkeley and Los Angeles, 1954-68.

Bache, Richard M. *The Latest Phase of the Great Pyramid Discussion*. Philadelphia, 1885.

Balkie, J. 'The Sphinx', in J.H. Hastings, *Encyclopedia of Religion and Ethics*. Vol. XI, pp. 767-8. Edinburgh, 1920.

Ballard, Robert T. *The Solution of the Pyramid Problem*. New York, 1882.

Bandelier, Adolf Francis. 'The Ruins at Piahuanaco', *American Antiquarian Society Proceedings*, XXI, pp. 218-65, 1911.

Bell, Edward. *The Architecture of Ancient Egypt*. London, 1915.

Benavides, Rudolfo. *Dramatic Prophecies of the Great Pyramids*. Mexico, 1961.

Bennett, Wendell C. 'Chavin Stone Carving', *Yale Anthropological Studies*. New Haven, Conn., 1942.

Bennett, Wendell C. 'Excavations at Tiahuanaco', *Anthropological*

Papers, American Museum of Natural History, Vol. 34, pp. 359-494. New York, 1934.

Bennett, Wendell C. (As Editor) 'A Reappraisal of Peruvian Arts', *Archeology Memoir* 4, Society for American Archeology. Menasha, 1948.

Blavatsky, Helena P. *Isis Unveiled*. Los Angeles, 1931.

Blavatsky, Helena P. *The Secret Doctrine*, 2 Vols. Los Angeles, 1930.

Breasted, James H. *A History of Egypt from the Earliest Times to the Persian Conquest*. New York, 1909.

Breasted, James H. *The Development of Religion and Thought in Ancient Egypt*. New York, 1912.

Bristowe, E.S.G. *The Man Who Built the Great Pyramid*, London, 1932.

Brooke, M.W.H.L. *The Great Pyramid at Gizeh*. London, 1908.

Brunton, Paul. *A Search in Secret Egypt*. London, 1936.

Bonwick, James. *Pyramid Facts and Fancies*, London, 1877.

Bothwell, A. *The Magic of the Pyramid*. Goose, 1915.

Boyce, Shirley. 'The Pyramid Pioneers Fire Safety', *Buildings*, Vol. 66, No. 6, June, 1972.

Burgoyne, Thomas H. *The Light of Egypt*. Denver, Colo., 1963.

Burgoyne, Thomas H. *The Holy Bible*. New York, 1901.

Caffery, Jefferson, and Boyer, David S. 'Fresh Treasures from Egypt's Ancient Sands', Vol. CVIII, No. 5, Nov., 1955.

deCampe, L. Sprague. 'How the Pyramids Were Built', *Fate*, Vol. 15, No. 12, Dec., 1962.

Carey, George W. *God-Man: The Word Made Flesh*. Los Angeles, Cal., 1920.

Cerny, J. *Ancient Egyptian Religion*. London, 1952.

Chapman, Arthur Wood. *The Prophecy of the Pyramid*. London, 1933.

Chapman, Francis W. *The Great Pyramid of Gizeh from the Aspect of Symbolism*. London, 1931.

Charroux, Robert. *One Hundred Years of Man's Unknown History*. New York, 1970.

Clarke, Somers and Reginald Engelbach. *Ancient Egyptian Masonry; The Burning Craft*. London, 1930.

Cole, J.H. *Determination of the Exact Size and Orientation of the Great Pyramid of Giza*. Cairo, 1925.

Corbin, Bruce. *The Great Pyramid, God's Witness in Stone*. Guthrie, Oklahoma, 1935.

Cormack, Maribell. *Imhotep, Builder in Stone*. New York, 1965.

Cottrell, Leonard. *The Mountains of Pharaoh*. London, 1956.

Cummings, Jennie, 'Pyramid Church'. *Houston Review*, Vol. 1, No. 4, Dec., 1973.

Cummings, Jennie. *The Pyramid Guide*, Nos. 1-2-4-5. Elsinore, Cal., 1973.

Darter, Frances M. *Our Bible in Stone*. Salt Lake City, 1931.

Davidson, David. *The Great Pyramid, Its Divine Message*. London, 1932.

Dunham, D. 'Building an Egyptian Pyramid', in *Archaeology*, 9 (1956), No. 3, pp. 159-65.

Edgar, Morton. *The Great Pyramid: Its Spiritual Symbolism*. Glasgow, 1924.

Edwards, I.E.S. *The Pyramids of Egypt*. Viking Press, 1972.

Edwards, I.E.S. *The Early Dynastic Period in Egypt*. Cambridge, 1964.

Emery, Walter B. *Archaic Egypt*. Baltimore, 1961.

Erman, A. *A Handbook of Egyptian Religion* (English Translation, by A.S. Griffth). London, 1907.

Evans, Alberts. 'Metaphysical Mysteries of the Great Pyramid'. *The Osteopathic Physician*, May, 1972.

Flanigan, G. Patrick. *The Pyramid and Its Relationship to Biocosmic Energy*, 1972.

Forlong, J.G.R. *Rivers of Life*, Vols. 1 and 2. London, 1883.

Forlong, J.G.R. *Science of Comparative Religions*. London, 1897.

Gardner, Martin. *Fads & Fallacies*. New York, 1957.

Garnier, Col. J. *The Great Pyramid: Its Builder and Its Prophecy*. London, 1912.

Ghunaim, Mohammed Z. *The Buried Pyramid*. New York, 1956.

Ghunaim, Mohammed Z. *The Lost Pyramid*. New York, 1956.

Goose, A.B. *The Magic of the Pyramids*. London, 1915.

Gordon, Cyrus H. *Before Columbus*. New York, 1971.

Gray, Julian Thorbirn. *The Authorship and Message of the Great Pyramid*. Cincinnati, 1953.

Grinsell, Leslie V. *Egyptian Pyramids*. Gloucester, 1947.

Hall, Manly P. *The Secret Teachings of All Ages*. Los Angeles, Cal., 1969.

Hayes, W.C. *The Sceptre of Egypt*, 2 Vols. New York, New York, and Cambridge, Massachusetts, 1935.

Haberman, Frederick. *The Great Pyramid's Message to America*. St

Petersberg, Florida, 1932.

Higgins, Godfrey. *Anacalypsis*, Vols 1 and 2. New York, 1965.

Hunt, Avery. 'Harnessing Pyramid Power, Pyramid Power?', *Newsday*, Monday 24 September, 1973.

Hurry, J.B. *Imhotep*. Oxford, 1926.

Ibek, Ferrand. *La Pyramide de Cheops a-t-elle livre son secret?*, Malines Celt, 1951.

James, T.G.H. *Myths and Legends of Ancient Egypt*. New York, 1972.

Jeffery, Edmond C. *The Pyramids and the Patriarchs*. New York, 1952.

Jeffers, James A. *The Great Sphinx Speaks to God's People*. Los Angeles, 1942.

Johnson, Fredrick (Editor). 'Radio Carbon Dating', *Memoirs of the Society of American Archaeology*, Salt Lake City, 1951.

Kellison, Cathrine. 'If Pyramids Could Talk ...!!!' *Playgirl*, November, 1973.

Kingsland, William. *The Great Pyramid in Fact and in Theory*. London, 1932.

Klein, H. Arthur. *Great Structures of the World*. New York, 1968.

Knight, Charles S. *The Mystery and Prophecy of the Great Pyramid*. San Jose, California, 1933.

Kolosimo, Peter. *Not of This World*. New York, 1973.

Kozyrev, Nikolai. 'Possibility of Experimental Study of the Properties of Time', Joint Publications Research Service, NTIS. Springfield, Virginia, 1968.

Kuhn, Alvin Boyd. *The Lost Light*. Columbia University, 1940.

Landone, Brown. *Prophecies of Melchi–Zedek in the Great Pyramid*. New York, 1940.

Lewis, Havre Spencer. *The Symbolic Prophecy of the Great Pyramid*. San Jose, California, 1936.

Lucas, A. *Ancient Egyptian Materials and Industries*, 4th edition revised by J.R. Harris. London, 1962.

Manning, Al G. 'Can Pyramid Power Work for You?' *Occult*, Vol. 4, No. 3, October, 1973.

Manning, Al G. 'How to Use the Mystic Pyramid'. Los Angeles, California, 1970.

Martin, Russ. 'Building the Great Pyramid 1973 A.D.'. *TWA Ambassador*, Vol. 6, No. 7, July, 1973.

Massey, Gerald. *The Natural Genesis*, Vols. 1 and 2. London, 1883.

Massey, Gerald. *Ancient Egypt*, Vols. 1 and 2. London, 1907.

Mercer, S.A.B. *The Pyramid Texts in Translation and Commentary*, 4 Vols. New York, 1952.

Mertz, Barbara. *Temples, Tombs and Hieroglyphs*. New York, 1964.

Montet, Pierre. *Eternal Egypt*. New York, 1964.

Neugebauer, O. *The Exact Sciences of Antiquity*. Princeton, 1951.

Norman, Ernest L. 'The Infinite Concept of Cosmic Creation', No. 2, Santa Barbara, California, 1960.

Norton, Roy. 'Monuments to UFO Space Pioneers', *Saga*, Vol. 44, No. 3, June, 1972.

Ostrander, Sheila. Schroeder, Lynn. *Psychic Discoveries Behind the Iron Curtain*. New York, 1970.

Owen, A.R.G. 'The Shapes of Egyptian Pyramids', *New Horizons*, Toronto, Canada, 1973.

Palmer, Ernest G. *The Secret of Ancient Egypt*. London, 1924.

Parker, Richard A. *The Calendars of Ancient Egypt*. Chicago, 1950.

Pawley, G.S. 'Do the Pyramids Show Continental Drift', *Science*, Vol. 179, March, 1973.

Petrie, W.M.F. *The Royal Tombs of the First Dynasty*, Part I. London, 1900.

Petrie, W.M.F. *The Royal Tombs of the Earliest Dynasties*, Part II. London, 1901.

Platt, Paul T. *Secret: The Pyramid and the Lisa*. New York, 1954.

Platt, Paul T. *The Secret of Secrets*. New York, 1955.

Platt, Paul T. *Psychic Observer*, Entire Issue, Vol. XXXIII, No. 7, Nov., 1972.

Platt, Paul T. *Pyramid News*, No. 7, September 26, 1973. (Edited by the Transamerican Corporation.)

Racey, Robert R. *The Gizeh Sphinx and Middle Egyptian Pyramids*. Winnipeg, Canada, 1937.

Rand, Howard B. *The Challenge of the Great Pyramid*. Haverhill, Massachusetts, 1943.

Rawlinson, G. *History of Herodotus* (Every Man's Library, edited by E.H. Blakney). London, 1912.

Reich, Wilhelm. 'Cosmic Superimposition', The Wilhelm Reich Foundation, Orgonon. Rangeley, Maine, 1951.

Reisner, G.A. *Mycerinus: the Temples of the Third Pyramid at Giza*. Cambridge, Massachusetts, 1931.

Reisner, G.A. *The Development of the Egyptian Tomb down to the Accession of Cheops*. Cambridge, Massachusetts, 1935.

Roberts, Jane. *The Seth Material.* Englewood Cliffs, New Jersey, 1970.

Robinson, Lytle. *The Great Pyramid and Its Builders.* Virginia Beach, 1966.

Russell, Walter. 'The Secret of Light', University of Science and Philosophy. Waynesboro, Virginia.

Rutherford, Adam. *Pyramidology.* Dunstable, Bedfordshire, 1961.

Riffert, G.R. *The Great Pyramid, Proof of God.* Haverhill, Massachusetts, 1944.

Rutherford, Adam. *Outline of Pyramidology.* London, 1957.

Schuré, Eduard. *The Mysteries of Ancient Egypt.* Hermes/Moses. Blauvet, New York, 1971.

Sendy, Jean. *Those Gods Who Made Heaven & Earth.* New York, 1972.

Shealy, Julian B. *The Key to Our God Given Heritage.* Columbia, South Carolina, 1967.

Shirota, Jon. 'Legacy of the Unknown', Vols. 1 and 2, March, 1973.

Sinnett, Alfred P. *The Pyramids and Stonehenge.* London, 1958.

Smith, E. Baldwin. *Egyptian Architecture as a Cultural Expression.* New York, 1938.

Smith, G.E. and Dawson, W.R. *Egyptian Mummies.* London, 1924.

Smith, Robert William. *Mysteries of the Ages.* Salt Lake City, 1936.

Smith, Warren. 'Mysterious Pyramids Around the World', *Saga*, Vol. 47, No. 1, October, 1973.

Smith, Worth. *The House of Glory.* New York, 1939.

Smith, William Stevenson. *Art & Architecture of Ancient Egypt.* Middlesex, 1958.

Smith, W. Stevenson. *A History of Egyptian Sculpture and Painting in the Old Kingdom.* Oxford, 1946.

Smith, W.S. *The Art and Architecture of Ancient Egypt* (The Pelican History of Art). London, 1958.

Stewart, Basil. *The Mystery of the Great Pyramid.* London, 1929.

Stewart, Basil. *The True Purpose of the Great Pyramid.* Exeter, 1935.

Straub, Walter L., *Anglo-Israel. Mysteries Unmasked.* Omaha, Nebraska, 1937.

Tellefsen, Olaf. 'A New Theory of Pyramid Building', *Natural History*, Vol. LXXIX, No. 9, November, 1970.

Thompson, J. Eric. *The Rise and Fall of Maya Civilization.* Norman, Okla., 1954.

Tompkins, Peter. *Secrets of the Great Pyramid.* New York, 1971.

Toth, Max. 'The Mysterious Pyramids', *Beyond Reality*, Vol. I, No. 2, December, 1972.

Touny, A.D. *Sport in Ancient Egypt.* Leipzig, 1969.

Tunstall, John. 'Pharaoh's Curse', Toronto Globe and Mail, July 30, 1969.

Tucker, William J. *Ptolemaic Astrology.* Sidcup, Kentucky, 1962.

Weeks, Kent and I.E.S. Edwards. 'The Great Pyramid Debate', *Natural History*, Vol. LXXIX, No. 10, December, 1970.

Vaillant, George C. *The Aztecs of Mexico.* New York, 1962.

Von Däniken, Erich. *Chariots of the Gods?* New York, 1970.

Vyse, H. and Perring, J.S. *Operations Carried out on the Pyramids of Gizeh*, 3 Vols. London, 1840-2.

Waddell, L.A. *Egyptian Civilization, Its Sumarian Origin and Real Chronology.* London, 1930.

Wheeler, N.F. 'Pyramids and Their Purpose', in *Antiquity*, IX (1935), pp. 172-85.

Winlock, H.E. *The Rise and Fall of the Middle Kingdom in Thebes.* New York, 1947.

Winlock, H.E. 'Pyramid Meditation', *National Enquirer*, Jan. 13, 1974.

Index

Index

Now read...

PENDULUM POWER

A mystery you can see, a power you can feel

The power of the pendulum has been used since the beginnings of time. Those with the knowledge of its use have located buried treasure, discovered hidden water, divined the future and reaped success of all kinds.

PENDULUM POWER teaches you how to use the pendulum, how to make your own and how its amazing powers can be put to use right away.

PENDULUM POWER reveals the mysterious origins of the pendulum, its application in love and sex, in choosing a diet or selecting a job, in finding lost objects and in healing.

PENDULUM POWER: YOUR ENTRANCE INTO THE WORLD OF INTUITIVE AWARENESS.